HOLLYWOOD
Rogues

Also published by St. Martin's Press:

The Hollywood Murder Casebook

HOLLYWOOD Rogues

MICHAEL MUNN

St. Martin's Press
New York

Library of Congress Cataloging-in-Publication Data

Munn, Michael.
    Hollywood rogues / by Michael Munn.
        p.   cm.
    "A Thomas Dunne book."
    ISBN 0-312-06995-2
    1. Motion picture actors and actresses—California—Los Angeles—
Anecdotes.   2. Hollywood (Los Angeles, Calif.)—Social life and
customs—Anecdotes.   I. Title.
PN2285.M86   1992
791.43′028′092279494—dc20
    [B]   91-38138
                                                                              CIP

First published in Great Britain by Robson Books Limited.

First U.S. Edition: April 1992
10 9 8 7 6 5 4 3 2 1

For Tony

Contents

HOLLYWOOD
Rogues

1

Boozing, Pill-popping Pioneers

Hollywood used to be such a quiet place. It was known as the
Frostless Belt. Groves of oranges and lemons blossomed in the
ever-warm Californian sun. Tourists came to luxuriate in the
peace and solitude of the valley. Then in came the movie
industry and out went the peace and quiet.

Cinema was in its infancy in 1907 when the Selig film
company moved into Los Angeles, right next door to
Hollywood, and other film companies from all over America
followed Selig's example.

But it is Cecil B De Mille who is generally given the credit
for turning Hollywood into a movie factory when, in 1913, he
filmed *The Squaw Man* there. By 1920 Hollywood was turning
out almost eight hundred films a year, and the word
'Hollywood' became a synonym for all the glamour,
professionalism and also the decadence that the film business
excelled in.

There were bound to be a few rogues let loose in
Hollywood. After all, it offered so much. There was plenty of
money to be earned by those who made it to the top – even by
those who only made it half way. That left the way open for a
little and more of what you fancy. For some, the pace and the

increasing demands set upon them to do better and climb higher ultimately led to a life of excess. And, for many, the desire for a little of whatever became a lust for more. Especially when money was no object.

Whatever the stars – the gods and goddesses of this new art form – were doing behind locked doors, the public were given to believe that there was no difference between the screen image and the real lives of the likes of Pearl White, Dustin Farnum, Mabel Normand, Charles Chaplin, Mary Pickford and Douglas Fairbanks.

In fact, the very thought that pure, virginal little Mary Pickford, for instance, could ever have been anything other than pure and virginal was unthinkable. So Adolph Zukor, head of Famous Players, who kept Pickford tied to a morally clean contract, dared not let the public know that she had in fact been married to actor and drunk Owen Moore since 1911.

Nor could the truth be revealed about Mary's brother, Jack. He had a somewhat chequered career as an actor, and was a true pioneering Hollywood Rogue, leading the way for others to follow and even excel when it came to boozing, pill-popping and coke-snorting. He was, as Donald Crisp once remarked, 'a drunk before he was a man'.

As a skinny youngster, he lived in the shadows of his demure sisters Mary and Lottie who effortlessly caught the attention of film makers. Intent on carving his own niche in movies he volunteered to double for his sisters, doing their stunts, like taking falls and riding horseback.

Film crews liked the spunky young kid and goaded him into drinking alcohol. To complete his initiation into manhood they took him off to a whorehouse. He resisted at first because, he admitted, he had not yet grown any pubic hair. Someone solved the ticklish problem by applying a moustache from the make-up department, providing him with a rich thatch which the girls at the brothel thought such a great gag that they gave him special attention.

By the age of fourteen, Jack Pickford was a veteran boozer and womanizer.

Jack wasn't the only Pickford with a penchant for strong liquor. His sisters liked it too. Mary, the most successful of the Pickfords, acquired the taste for alcohol from her husband, and because her career depended totally on her screen image of total innocence she was forced to do all her drinking in secret. And her loving. It was worrying enough for Zukor that she was married, but when she began a love affair with dashing Douglas Fairbanks in 1915 it could easily have been the end of both Pickford's and Fairbanks's careers. When they married in 1920, Hollywood held its breath to see how the public responded. And to everyone's great relief the fans approved.

Jack's career, while never reaching the heights of Mary's, served him well. He was by no stretch of the imagination like his characters on screen. He specialized in Tom Sawyer-type roles, never giving even the merest hint of his real-life excesses. Those who knew him well knew of his indulgences in booze and sex. Director Eddie Sutherland summed up his lifestyle with 'What do you expect from a guy with the biggest thirst and the biggest joint in town? Join a monastery?'

He seemed to overcome his playboy image when he fell in love and married Olive Thomas. This delighted the fans. To them he was the 'Ideal American Boy'. She was the 'Ideal American Girl'. Together they were 'The Ideal Couple'. But ordinary Mr and Mrs America hadn't a clue what the Ideal Couple were up to.

Olive was indeed the 'ideal' girl for roguish Jack. A runaway and a teenage bride for a short while, Olive shared Jack's taste for the fruits of Hollywood – and they weren't the kind that grew in the frost-free valleys. By 1916 a new 'lift' had emerged among certain quarters of the Hollywood ravers. Cocaine, or 'joy powder', was being passed at parties. Among the partakers were Jack and Olive.

Not surprisingly, theirs was a marriage as stormy as Cape Horn. Having both been too busy filming when they married, their honeymoon had been indefinitely postponed. In September 1920 when their marriage was at a particularly low ebb, they decided it was time to take that much missed honeymoon in Paris. What occurred there was the first major scandal to rock Hollywood; not surprisingly the actual facts are a little vague due to the many rumours and, no doubt, a certain amount of covering up.

It seems that Olive went on to Paris, not entirely alone, while Jack remained in Hollywood to complete *The Little Shepherd of Kingdom Come.* Olive's travelling companion was none other than Mr Mary Pickford, the ever-drunk Owen Moore, whose alcoholic condition had increased with his wife's rejection of him in favour of Fairbanks. Jack joined them shortly after.

On the morning of 20 September the naked body of Olive Thomas was found in the Royal Suite of the Hotel Crillon. Clutched in her hand was a bottle of toxic bichloride.

The Ideal Girl had committed suicide. But Jack refuted the suicide verdict, maintaining that, following an evening spent in Parisian cafés, she had taken the tablets by mistake.

Mary came to his aid and issued a statement denying the 'sickening aspersions' on her brother's character, which ranged from claims that he was a drug addict to the theory that he had poisoned her for her various infidelities. In all this, Owen Moore had not a thing to say.

As Olive's final steps were traced on that fateful evening, a more lurid succession of activities than merely visiting cafés was revealed. Olive, alone, had been seen in some of the French capital's meanest dives with notorious underworld figures. It was suggested that she was desperately trying to secure large quantities of heroin, possibly for Jack, maybe for herself, but had failed. Unable to make it through the night, she took the mercury tablets.

Adding fuel to the flames of this particular fire, an investigation by the United States Government into the drug smuggling operation of a Captain Spaudling of the United States Army revealed that Olive Thomas was one of the Captain's customers.

Mary helped Jack to pick up the pieces after Olive's funeral by finding him work to keep him occupied. But Jack was hell-bent on a wild life. In 1921 he was arrested on a driving charge and lost his licence.

He got married to Marilyn Miller, divorced her, and married Mary Mulhern. Like Olive, they were former Follies girls. 'One thing he could do,' remarked his lawyer Paul O'Brien, 'was marry beautiful women.'

Mary dreaded him turning up in his usual drunken state at her legendary home, Pickfair. On one occasion he arrived for a formal party with Bea Lillie, an English musical comedy star. The loaded couple walked arm in arm with mock dignity straight into the swimming pool.

His last film was *Gang War* in 1928. That year his beloved mother died, and, unable to cope with the bereavement, he gave up work altogether. He wasted away from dissipation over the next five years and died aged only thirty-five.

Not all Hollywood drinkers were that self-destructive, Harry B Warner was the kind of rogue people loved. Despite Warner's binges, Cecil B De Mille was confident enough that his acting abilities and professionalism would overcome his attachment to the bottle to have him portray Christ in the 1927 epic *The King of Kings*. Jesse Lasky Jnr, whose father was vice-president of Paramount and a friend of De Mille, told me what happened.

H B Warner didn't drag people down with him, or mix with the kind of people who could drag him down, and he survived a career that spanned more than forty years. Warner had taken an oath to my father and to Cecil B De Mille not to indulge during the filming of *The King of Kings*, and for a while he kept his word. But whether it was the pressure of playing such a lofty role or just the fact that he desperately missed a drop or two, midway through filming he began to hit the bottle.

He was an actor of some dignity, despite his forays into saloons, but he was not one to willingly endure the kind of lengthy sermons which De Mille delivered from a pulpit to his cast one day on the meaning of the New Testament. After more than a hour of listening to De Mille's pious promotion, Warner fell asleep on Judas's shoulder.

Now, De Mille had problems enough without having his Jesus drinking. Many at that time thought it blasphemous for any actor to portray Christ, and De Mille was very careful to shield Warner from prying and sanctimonious eyes. Warner arrived each day at the studio in a car with the blinds down, and then left the car for his dressing room wearing a veil. On location Warner had to eat alone in his tent. Only the most resolute efforts by De Mille and his chief publicist, Barrett Kiesling, kept the news that the screen Jesus was an alcoholic a secret.

One day Warner went missing from the location. De Mille went off in hot pursuit and discovered Warner, in the robes of the Saviour, knocking back a bottle of whisky. It was a mark of De Mille's fondness for Warner, who appeared throughout his career in C B's pictures, that he didn't fire him. Besides, if he'd fired Warner he would have only courted the kind of publicity he was desperate to avoid on this picture.

One actor who didn't give a damn what people thought about his behaviour was John Barrymore. He enjoyed his greatest triumphs on the stage rather than on film, and few of his many movies linger in the mind.

Barrymore had intended to become either a journalist, a painter or commercial artist, as did his brother Lionel. But John didn't make any great strides in either field, so in 1903 his sister, the actress Ethel, secured him a small part in a play she was appearing in, and he was set on a whole new career. Later that year he made his Broadway début in *Glad of It* by which time he was already drinking heavily.

He made his film début in 1913 in *An American Citizen* but

continued to return to the stage – and to the bottle. It was in 1924 that he became part of the star system when Warners took him under contract for $76,250 a picture, plus an extra $7,625 a week if the filming went over the allotted seven-week schedule, plus all expenses. He made his few most memorable films for Warners, including *The Sea Beast* and *Don Juan*. Then, in 1926, he moved over to United Artists for $100,000 a film, plus a share of the profits when he played the eponymous hero in *The Beloved Rogue*. But his film career never did reach great heights after that, although he continued to work steadily in pictures. And The Beloved Rogue proved to be not quite so beloved after all.

The problem with Barrymore was that he enjoyed being considered a rogue. He generally gave his greatest performances, not in the theatre or in the studio, but in saloons. He preferred to work with as little effort as possible, saving his energy and vigour for drinking, carousing and womanizing, excelling in all three activities.

In 1928 he was to be seen at the Plantation Club, owned by Fatty Arbuckle, where Barrymore, with vast amounts of whisky inside him, camped it up on the stage with Jackie Coogan who had been *The Kid* opposite Chaplin.

By 1932, at the age of forty and under contract to MGM, he was a fading matinée idol and an alcoholic. His behaviour became ever more outrageous. A producer's wife at a Hollywood party went to the ladies and found Barrymore peeing in a corner of the room. 'Mr Barrymore, this is for ladies,' remarked the shocked lady, who was even more shocked when Barrymore held out his pecker and replied, 'So, madam, is this!'

His drinking caused delays on sets and his memory was faltering. Cue cards had to be held up for him. Midway during filming on *Romeo and Juliet*, the forty-four-year-old Romeo became so drunk he was incapable of working. The role was offered to William Powell who graciously refused the part because Barrymore had given him his start in films. So when Barrymore was sober enough he returned to the set. After the film was completed he entered a clinic to be treated for alcoholism.

RKO gave him a chance when director Worthington Miner persuaded studio head Pandro S Berman to cast him in *Hat, Coat and Glove*. Berman was at first hesitant, but Miner convinced him he could handle Barrymore. The first week's shooting went well. Barrymore behaved and responded to Miner's direction. Then one day Barrymore took the film crew to lunch. The crew came back but Barrymore didn't. He'd simply decided he didn't want to do the film anymore, and nothing the studio could do or say would entice him back. They managed to retrieve some of the money they'd paid him through insurance and then recast his part with Ricardo Cortez.

He was relegated to B-pictures at major studios and major films at small studios. In 1939 an up-and-coming screen writer, Garson Kanin, was promised by his boss, Pandro S Berman, that he could direct any film of his choosing. Kanin chose *The Great Man Votes*, a story RKO had shelved. Berman agreed, but when Kanin told him he wanted John Barrymore to be the star, Berman turned white and said, 'He's not going to work on this lot. He's unreliable and irresponsible and impossible. The last time we let that bastard on the lot, we didn't want him but this big director from New York had the same bee in his bonnet you've got.'

Kanin persisted and Pandro relented. The deal was set up and filming commenced with Garson directing a seemingly amiable and willing Barrymore. By and large the filming was without trouble, but Barrymore insisted that blackboards with all his dialogue written on be placed strategically about the set. When asked why he had to rely on idiot boards, Barrymore replied, 'My memory is full of beauty: Hamlet's soliloquies, Queen Mab's speech, the Song of Solomon. Do you expect me to clutter up all that with this horse shit?'

Kanin tolerated the idiot boards until he came to shoot a scene in which Barrymore had only one word to utter: 'Yes'. He insisted the word be written on a blackboard. On the verge of losing his temper, Kanin said, 'Be reasonable, Mr Barrymore. You're asked "Are you Gregory Vance?" And you *are*, so what else could you possibly say?'

'Well,' replied Barrymore thoughtfully, 'I could say "No", and then where would you be?'

The blackboard was held up for Barrymore to read from.

That small incident was overshadowed only by Barrymore's outburst when ten-year-old actress Virginia Weilder effortlessly upstaged him during one of his important speeches.

'What the hell do you think you're doing, you hammy little bitch?' he yelled at her. In his rage, he picked her up and threw the terrified moppet across the set, to be caught, fortunately, by stage hands. Barrymore's rage knew no bounds. 'Who the hell do you think you're acting with, you silly little brute?' he ranted.

Kanin tried to calm him down, but Barrymore was in a tempestuous fury. 'I've messed it up with bitches like her before,' he raged. Filming was abandoned for the duration of the day, and the scene was redone the following morning. The girl didn't so much as twitch a muscle, and Barrymore finished the scene perfectly without further trouble.

He returned to the stage in 1939 in *My Dear Children* with his fourth wife, Elaine Barrie. It ran for thirty-four weeks in Chicago and moved to New York in 1940. In both cities audiences flocked to the play – but they came mainly to see Barrymore forgetting his lines and sometimes falling over. During a performance in Chicago he literally collapsed on stage and had to be taken to hospital. Rumours of a fatal stroke reached Hollywood. Garson Kanin sent a telegram to the hospital enquiring after him. Barrymore reassured his friend by telegram: DON'T WORRY. FOR A MAN WHO HAS BEEN DEAD FOR FIFTEEN YEARS I AM IN REMARKABLE HEALTH.

He weathered numerous stormy love affairs, including four marriages. He didn't trust women. He became, in his final years, somewhat embittered about love and women. In an interview, Anthony Quinn who idolized Barrymore, described his hero's attitude to women. 'He told me not to trust any woman. He said to me, "Women, they're all twittering vaginas." So I said to him, "How come you married so many times then?" and he said, "Because I loved the cunts." '

His last years were spent mainly in B-films parodying himself as a broken-down, drunken ham. He ignored his doctor's orders to stop drinking. The older he got, the more cynical he became, and the more people came to detest him. Paul D O'Brien, a Hollywood attorney, said of Barrymore, 'That man was so vulgar and vicious that even his make-up man would walk away from him.'

The few friends he had loved him. His closest friends included W C Fields, himself a legendary drunk, and artist John Decker. 'The people – the men – he loved,' said Anthony Quinn, 'he called "shits", like John Decker, W C Fields, Thomas Mitchell and Gene Fowler. I was very happy when he started calling me a "shit".'

For hours each evening Barrymore and his 'shits' would sit, talk and drink. Often they'd go to Earl Carroll's night club on Sunset Boulevard, a huge place seating around 2,500 and featuring some of Hollywood's most beautiful female singers.

Barrymore never dressed for the occasion and he had to borrow a tie on the door to be allowed inside. During one visit he was pressed by the Master of Ceremonies to dance with what the MC described as 'the most beautiful Earl Carroll girl'. Instead, Barrymore found himself sweeping the floor with an exceedingly ugly, over-painted woman. The audience roared with laughter at the sight of the fading star being made a fool of this way.

When the dance was over, Barrymore graciously kissed the woman's hand, went over to the microphone and said, 'As for you, ladies and gentlemen, you can all go fuck yourselves.'

The house in which he lived was constantly being extended. He believed that if he ever stopped building he would die, a compulsion inherited by Anthony Quinn. During Quinn's first visit to Barrymore's house, he was led into the den where Barrymore proceeded to urinate into a sink. An indication, perhaps, that Barrymore was well and truly pissed off. This peculiar behaviour did nothing to dispel Quinn's undying admiration for Barrymore, who died penniless in 1942; a not unsurprising end for a hard-drinking and not altogether beloved rogue who was in fact just one, albeit the most famous, of a hard-drinking dynasty.

His father, Maurice Barrymore, was in real life Herbert Albert Blythe, an amateur middleweight boxing champion of England who discovered he had a hidden talent for acting. He set sail for New York and became a popular actor, calling himself Maurice Barrymore, and married America's top comedienne Georgina Drew. When she died Maurice suffered bouts of violent depression and took to hitting the bottle with a vengeance.

He ended his days in 1905, aged fifty-eight, in a clinic where he was being treated for alcoholism and insanity. His son, John Barrymore, inherited his father's whisky-soaked mantle which was then passed down to John Drew Barrymore Jnr.

Born in 1932, John Junior also took to treading the boards but he was forever overshadowed by his father's huge talent. That was reason enough for John Junior to drink heavily. He had a stormy first marriage to Cara Williams and on one occasion he beat her up. He even beat up the police who came to rescue her. When they overpowered him he was carted off to jail.

He married three times – his second marriage was postponed after a court case in which he was charged with brawling – and he was a regular visitor to the courts, usually on drink-driving charges. He was even banned from acting because of his drunken behaviour.

John Junior's daughter, Drew Barrymore, was the seven-year-old starlet of *ET* in 1982. By the time she was nine she was drinking. At the age of ten she was smoking pot, and by her twelfth birthday she was using cocaine. At fourteen she was a reformed alcoholic-addict.

John Barrymore had a daughter, Diana, who, like her brother John Junior, turned to acting *and* to drink. She also married three times and was arrested on numerous occasions on charges ranging from drunken brawls to shoplifting. She always blamed her condition on her father's neglect.

Her desperation became such that she tried to end it all by downing 27 sleeping tables with whisky, but survived after being treated in a nursing home. She joined Alcoholics Anonymous, but was a lost cause. In 1957 she was found dead in her New York home at the age of thirty-eight.

John Barrymore's brother, Lionel, was the black sheep of the family. He didn't drink to excess and didn't get himself arrested or fired from studios. He was most famous for playing Dr Gillespie in all fifteen of the *Dr Kildare* films. He continued to act and remain sober even after a paralysing fall confined him to a wheelchair for the rest of his life, until he passed away in 1954 aged seventy-six. Not surprisingly, John and his brother Lionel spent little time socializing together. John preferred the company of his boozing buddies.

One of the Barrymore clan of happy hour habitués, W C Fields, managed to survive a little longer than most with a penchant for hard liquor. He was in real life, as on the screen, a thorough rogue. He generally bragged, cheated, conned, lied and drank his way through the plots of his films. Off screen, he was regarded as being remarkably like his film persona, and maybe even more aggressive.

He came from a background of exceptional hardship that no doubt contributed to his comedic beliefs and life style. He ran away from home when he was eleven after a violent fight with his father. He lived rough and alone, suffering cold after cold resulting in his rasping wheeze. His many fights (along with generous doses of liquor) helped to produce the famous bulbous nose. For months the young Fields avoided starvation by landing odd jobs and stealing. He spent many a night in jail.

He had taught himself to juggle by the age of nine, and at fourteen was hired as a juggler in an amusement park. He became a vaudeville headliner at the age of twenty and from there went on to become an actor on Broadway, scoring a huge success in *Poppy* on Broadway in 1923. Two years later he starred in the film adaptation, retitled *Sally of the Sawdust*, and his film career was off and running. Because of his theatrical ability, he managed the transition from silent screen to talkies effortlessly. Talking films enabled him to convey even more pointedly his mistrust of authority, his flagrant contempt for the institution of the family and a deep suspicion of his fellow man. His fans never knew that his screen attitudes reflected his personal beliefs.

He particularly distrusted banks and the men who ran them. This led him to deposit his savings in small amounts all over the world. He had something like seven hundred savings accounts under a huge variety of aliases in many countries.

He didn't leave many tips at the bars or the restaurants he drank in. According to director Joseph L Mankiewicz, who wrote the screenplay of a Fields film, *Million Dollar Legs* (1932), Fields was 'one of the meanest human beings who ever lived'.

W C had a contempt bordering on hatred for almost anyone. One night he met Greg La Cava, a famous director in the thirties, in a café. Cava said, 'Congratulate me. I've just signed a new five-year deal at RKO.'

'You can't work for RKO,' said Fields. 'The goddamned place is run by Jews.'

'What are you talking about?' replied Cava. 'George Schaefer [then head of RKO] is a Catholic.'

'Catholics,' Fields responded, 'are the worst kind of Jews.'

Paramount, who had Fields under contract, made him promise that during the three or four weeks prior to shooting on a picture, he would lay off the booze. Fields vowed that instead of drinking he would play golf. Two Paramount executives watched him play eighteen holes daily. What they didn't see what that his golf bag was filled with beer.

In 1936 he remade *Poppy*, this time retaining the play's original title, but his heavy drinking made him seriously ill during much of the filming, and the director had to resort to using a stand-in. His poor health kept him off the screen for two years, and his friends realized just how ill he was when he managed to give up drinking for a whole year.

He returned in *The Big Broadcast* in 1938. He looked years older and his bulbous nose had taken on a darker shade of purple. But he wasn't too ill to fight with Paramount over money, demanding a rise which the studio refused him. So he went to Universal where they were prepared to pay him $125,000 per film plus $25,000 for outlining each story. Universal came to discover just how difficult Fields was to work with, but, like his former studio, they recognized that there was a cult following out there, and Fields was allowed to turn out four films that pleased his following and remain among his most popular.

The first of these, *You Can't Cheat an Honest Man* (1939), was not finished without the kind of trouble Universal would learn to expect from a Fields vehicle. George Marshall, a tough director of countless westerns, gave up trying to direct the perpetually pissed W C, so Fields's friend Edward Cline was brought in to finish the job.

Then came *My Little Chickadee*, which teamed Fields with the incomparable Mae West. The deal was set for them to collaborate on the script, but Fields didn't collaborate with anything but a bottle. Mae West said of him: 'There is no one quite like Bill. And it would be snide of me to add *Thank God*. A great performer. My only doubts about him come in bottles.'

There followed *The Bank Dick* in 1940 and *Never Give a Sucker an Even Break* in 1941. But despite their enormous appeal Universal decided it was now time to wash their hands of the drunk and difficult Fields.

He tried to find work elsewhere, but his reputation was well ahead of him. Although ill with polyneuritis, he began drinking even *more*. Twentieth Century-Fox gave him a chance in 1942 with a one-scene-only cameo appearance in *Tale of Manhattan* He blew it and the scene was cut from the release print.

Fields always said he hated Christmas. By a twist of fate as cruel as he could be, he died on Christmas Day in 1946.

There was a premature and booze-sodden end for poor John Gilbert, one of MGM's biggest stars of the silent era. In 1928 he was the highest-paid star, receiving $10,000 a week. At his zenith he was a thorough professional, never turning up late for work, and drinking no more than anyone else in Hollywood. That was, until he was struck by three thunderous blows.

The first blow came from the stunning Swede, Greta Garbo. Despite the denials at the time, and for many years after, she and Gilbert had a passionate love affair. Gilbert was an immaculate leading man. Garbo was a cool Swede. Journalist Adela Rogers St Johns recalled, 'I have never seen two people so violently, excitedly in love.'

When they embraced in films like *Flesh and the Devil* and *A Woman of Affairs* the passion they displayed was for real. They made plans to get married. (He had already been married twice, the last time to actress Leatrice Joy, 1923-24.) It was to be a lavish double wedding – a true Hollywood double bill, with Gilbert marrying Garbo and director King Vidor marrying actress Eleanor Boardman. But Garbo didn't show, and the rejected Gilbert took solace in a bottle.

The second blow came from Wall Street in 1929. Like many others with too much money to spend, Gilbert invested, none too wisely, in stocks. After Garbo's rebuff, he had impetuously married Ina Claire. As he was returning from a honeymoon overseas he heard the news about the crash on Wall Street. Arriving back in America he discovered he had lost all his investments. He was broke.

Fortunately, he had a solid gold contract with MGM, but after his first performance in a talkie, *His Glorious Night*, had drawn guffaws from the audience, his fate was sealed. The third blow had been struck.

Knowing the devastating effect his first talkie was likely to have on his career, Gilbert turned up at the studio daily, whether he was called or not. Louis B Mayer was by now bent on ridding the studio of Gilbert and put every obstacle in his way, even ordering the gateman to fail to recognize the highly recognizable Gilbert. Such humiliation increased his already considerable drinking habit.

After a short succession of poor films, John Gilbert, in a drunken stupor, placed the following ad in the Hollywood trade press: 'Metro-Goldwyn-Mayer will neither offer me work nor release me from my contract. Signed, John Gilbert.'

When his contract with MGM finished, they refused to sign him up again. His career was over, as was his marriage to Ina Claire, and he had married yet again, to Virginia Bruce. Then Greta Garbo came to his rescue, but all she really succeeded in doing was rub salt in the wounds. She had been cast in the title role of *Queen Christina* and she insisted Metro give her Gilbert for her leading man. The poor man to whom Garbo had made it clear that she wanted to be alone now found himself in close proximity with the woman he had so passionately loved and who was now having to save him from a sinking career. Despite the film's success, it did nothing to help Gilbert regain his self-confidence. It just drove him further towards a self-willed end.

Gilbert's next and last film was *The Captain Hates the Sea* in 1935 in which he was fourth billed as a cynical, embittered, drunken Hollywood hack. He was virtually acting himself. He spent the first week of shooting on the wagon, but soon began drinking again, and was a thorough mess throughout filming and was difficult to handle. He ended his days a totally different man from the one who had once been a true gentleman of the silent screen. He became his own most destructive enemy and drank himself to death in 1936, aged thirty-nine.

That same year, the body of James Murray was found floating in the Hudson River in a re-creation of a suicide attempt scene from the film that had shot him to stardom, *The Crowd*, in 1928. The film's director, King Vidor, had personally chosen

Murray, who was an extra and bit-part player at MGM, for the lead. Suddenly he was a star, and Metro put him opposite Joan Crawford in *Rose Marie*. It was all a little too heady for Murray, who celebrated his sudden stardom by turning himself into a virtual overnight alcoholic. He began turning up late for work – sometimes he didn't turn up at all. He had trouble remembering his lines, and now with talking films, an actor who had difficulty delivering dialogue wasn't destined to survive.

Murray plummeted from sudden dizzying heights into obscurity. But one man still had faith in Murray. King Vidor wanted him to star in *Our Daily Bread* in 1933. But nobody knew where Murray was. He had disappeared. Then, one day, Vidor was asked in the street by a bum for money to buy a meal. It was James Murray. Vidor took him straight to the Brown Derby for dinner and asked him if he could pull himself together and take the lead in *Our Daily Bread*. Murray was enthusiastic until Vidor said, 'You'll have to quit drinking.'

Murray blew his top. 'Just because I stop you on the street and try to borrow a buck, you think you can tell me what to do. You know what you can do with your lousy part.'

Murray stormed out, never to be seen again by Vidor.

He managed to make two more films before he repeated for real a moment from *The Crowd* in which he had tried to commit suicide by leaping into a river from a bridge. In the scene, one of the most emotional ever filmed for a silent picture, he had been stopped by his screen son. In Murray's real life, there was no one to beg him not to do it.

While Murray and Gilbert were meeting their tragic ends, audiences around the world were laughing at the hysterical antics of a group of kids brought together by Hal Roach as *Our Gang*, a series of comedy shorts that had first appeared in 1922. With the coming of sound, and the passing of time, members of the Gang changed. By the thirties, among the most popular 'Little Rascals', as they later came to be known, were Spanky McFarland, Dickie Moore, Scotty Beckett and the unforgettable freckle-faced Carl 'Alfalfa' Switzer. They were all cute kids, but as they grew up, not all of them found themselves on the right side of the tracks.

Take Scotty Beckett. He was only three when he made his début in *Our Gang* in 1932. He graduated to adolescent roles in films like *King's Row* and *The Jolson Story*, but by the time he was nineteen he was drinking, and was arrested for drunken driving in 1948. It was just the first in a long line of run-ins with the law. In 1954 he was arrested for carrying a concealed weapon, and in 1957 he was arrested at the Mexican border and charged with possession of hard drugs.

In 1960 he attacked his stepdaughter with a crutch and was sent to jail for 180 days. He had made his last film, *Three For Jamie* in 1956, his first in five years. His career over and his young life in ruins, he slashed his wrists in 1962, survived and recovered to take a fatal overdose of sleeping pills in 1968 at the age of thirty-eight.

Carl Switzer found his career deteriorating as he got older. To supplement his income he became a hunting and fishing guide in northern California and later worked as a bartender. In 1959, after too many drinks, he got into a fight with a former hunting friend over a $50 debt. During the drunken brawl, a gun went off and thirty-three-year-old 'Alfalfa' dropped dead. The slaying was ruled 'justifiable homicide'.

This, perhaps, was the sort of behaviour one might expect from the Dead End Kids, that rabble of East Side punks who began in gangster films like *Dead End* (1937) opposite Bogart, and *Angels With Dirty Faces* (1938) opposite Cagney, and went on to star in their own series. On screen these kids kissed the ground that the mobsters walked on. They were just actors of course, but Leo Gorcey, who inherited the mantle of leader as the series progressed, carried his little tough punk image into real life and had several brushes with the law. He died in 1969, aged fifty-four. The original leader, Billy Halop, left the series in the early forties hoping to make it as a star in his own right. But he was an alcoholic and a has-been by the time he died in

1976, aged fifty-six.

One of the best-loved drunks was Spencer Tracy. He was loved because he was the actors' actor. Most Hollywood actors, even today, regard him as the screen's finest actor. But he could be hell to work with. His stubbornness, smugness and heavy drinking brought him into conflict with his co-stars, directors and crew.

Following a huge argument with producer Winfield Sheehan at the Twentieth Century-Fox studios in 1933, Tracy got drunk and passed out on a sofa on one of the sets. Sheehan had him locked in the sound stage, thinking it would be safer for Tracy and everybody else. The next morning Sheehan came on to the sound stage to find the film set in a complete shambles. Tracy had smashed everything up, including thousands of dollars' worth of lighting equipment. But despite such outbreaks, Tracy's method of 'natural acting' was one a good many up-and-coming younger actors tried to emulate.

It was during those Golden Days in the thirties that on to the Hollywood scene came someone who was to prove to be the biggest rogue of all – Errol Flynn.

Flynn was an expert in just about every form of excess, and drink and drugs were just the tip of the iceberg. When Warner Bros brought him across the Atlantic in style in 1935, Flynn began his Hollywood sojourn the way he intended it to go on – in the bar. With Warners paying his every expense, Flynn ordered 'only the best champagne, sport'.

In 1935 Warner Bros planned to film a lavish swashbuckler, *Captain Blood*, with Robert Donat in the title role. But Donat dropped out at the last minute and a massive search for a replacement took place until Hungarian director Michael Curtiz chose Errol Flynn. Studio head Jack Warner wasn't impressed with their new star when he saw the early rushes. Flynn was drunk. Warner told him, 'No one drinks at Warner Bros.' In saying that, Warner had unwittingly declared war on Flynn.

Flynn was also at war with Curtiz, who directed most of Flynn's best films and who was considered by actors and crew something of a dictator who ruled over his films with an iron rod. The fun-loving Flynn was destined to clash with the tyrannical Curtiz. During *Captain Blood* Curtiz tried to stop Flynn being too theatrical with subtle words of encouragement like, 'Stop acting like a goddamn faggot, you no good bum sonofabitch.'

To which Flynn responded with equal subtlety, 'Go fuck yourself, you dumb Hungarian.'

Their slanging matches continued throughout their association and one can only wonder at how they managed to produce such successful results on the screen. When news reached Flynn that Curtiz was to direct him in *The Adventures of Robin Hood* (1938), he was decidedly depressed at the prospect. On the first day of shooting, Flynn turned up an hour late and completely ignored Curtiz's 'Good morning, Flynn.'

The scene they were shooting was the classic banquet hall. Flynn went through his paces with less than enthusiasm, and when he had to knock back a goblet of soda pop, he spat it out and cried, 'Christ, where did you get this panther piss?'

Curtiz furiously yelled at Flynn that he had ruined the take at great cost, to which Flynn responded by tossing the remaining contents of the goblet in Curtiz's face.

Flynn continued drinking heavily and was usually joined in a binge by his co-star Alan Hale. As the days dragged on Flynn kept forgetting his lines, and every scene had to be reshot half a dozen times.

Jack Warner threatened to fire Flynn, who calmly replied, 'Sorry, sport, but I think I have a contract.'

Flynn's heavy drinking, and his use of cocaine, kif, opium and hashish, were met by ill health; he suffered all kinds of ailments, including sinusitis, gonorrhoea, emphysema, chronic irritation of the urethra, a heart murmur and tuberculosis in his right lung. While making *Desperate Journey* in 1942, he drank too much, ate too little and suffered from sleepless, headache-ridden nights.

With so much of his strength debilitated by booze, drugs and illness, it's a wonder he managed to find the vigour for the young girls he had such a taste for. One such girl was seventeen-year-old Nora Eddington whom he met in 1942 and who refused to sleep with him until one night, full of cocaine and alcohol, Flynn brutally raped her. She became pregnant, but refused to have an abortion, as Flynn suggested, because she was a Catholic. She insisted that Flynn marry her so their child could have a name; then, she said, he would be free to divorce her (even though she was a Catholic).

Oddly enough, he agreed to the marriage but refused to consider a divorce. However, he made sure she knew that he was intent on pursuing his accustomed lifestyle. They were married in 1943 in Acapulco in secret. He didn't want news of his marital status leaked, for fear it would ruin his affairs. He left his wife in Mexico, returning from his sexual adventures when she gave birth to their daughter, Deirdre.

It wasn't the womanizing that ended their marriage but his constant drug-taking. In his drugged state he often beat Nora, never able later to recall his violence towards her. He tried to go cold turkey in an effort to save their marriage, but that only made him worse. He always said he could give it up any time he liked. He was wrong. He was an addict and had become dependent on drugs.

Often Nora had to sponge Flynn down when he started to shake. When he reached for the morphine to inject himself she would straddle him and pin him down. Once he tried to inject her. This incident caused her to attempt suicide but Flynn managed to save her before she could knock back a deadly overdose of pills. That ended the marriage and they divorced in 1948.

That year he made *Don Juan* and promised director Vincent Sherman that he would behave. 'Forget all that stuff you've heard about me,' he told Sherman. 'I'll be on time and know all my lines.'

During the filming news reached him that his latest release *Escape Me Never* had been panned by the critics, and he began hitting the bottle hard again. Warner had forbidden him to take drugs or to drink during filming, but Flynn managed to mix cocaine with water and used it on his sinuses from an eye dropper. He had a friend bring him soup for lunch, the ingredients of which included a generous dose of vodka. That ended his days at Warners, and he was all but washed up.

He could behave when he wanted to. When he made *Against All Flags* at Universal in 1952, he stayed sober and turned up on time every day – but only because he was on a percentage of the picture's profits with no salary up front. On the first day of his next picture, *The Master of Ballantrae*, at Elstree in England, he turned up at the studio, went straight to the bar and downed six neat scotches.

He stayed on in Europe for a few more unmemorable pictures, including two for British film producer-director Herbert Wilcox, who thought his filmstar wife Anna Neagle and Flynn would make a dashing screen couple. Both films, *Lilacs in the Spring* and *King's Rhapsody*, proved as poisonous at the box office as the stuff Flynn was injecting himself with. As Anna Neagle told me:

I'm sure the only reason he agreed to do those pictures was because he needed the money. On *Lilacs in the Spring* he was splendid, and on *King's Rhapsody* he was murder. When he was sober he was a delight to work with. He learned his dance steps like lightning but on his bad days I can't remember anyone so terrible. He arrived for work no earlier than noon, unchanged and unshaved, just in time for the picnic lunch that had been provided for the cast.

One day he invited Herbert and myself on to his yacht, the *Zaca*, and he got terribly drunk and had a fight with his captain. They knocked each other about all over the deck.

During his last years he attempted to prove himself as an actor. He received excellent notices for *The Sun Also Rises* in

1957, and then turned in a fine performance in a role he was born for – portraying his boozy idol John Barrymore in *Too Much, Too Soon* (1958). By the time he came to make *The Roots of Heaven* in Africa, however, he was physically fading fast. The film's director, John Huston, described Flynn's condition to me:

> Errol was ill with a vastly enlarged liver, and he continued to drink and take drugs. He knew he was ill but put on a great show of good spirits.
>
> Night after night he sat alone in the middle of the compound with a book and with a bottle of vodka beside him. He was there when I went to sleep, and when I'd wake up in the middle of the night I'd see him still sitting there. The book was open but he wasn't reading any longer. I think he was just looking into his future, maybe knowing there wasn't much left of it.
>
> The company doctor came round to see me one day and said that he wasn't going to give Errol any more drugs. It was, he felt, a matter of ethics and he was prepared to be fired over it. So Errol found himself another doctor – a French army doctor – who was unconcerned with such things as ethics.

Flynn claimed he survived the ordeal of filming in Africa by drinking only vodka and fruit juice. In the finished picture Flynn was visibly bloated and looked much older than he was.

Jack Warner described him at that time as 'one of the living dead'.

Flynn made his last film, *Cuban Rebel Girls*, in 1959, a peculiar tribute to Fidel Castro which he wrote, co-produced and narrated. He returned to Los Angeles where Nora, who had remained friends with him, saw him having to be assisted off the plane. He was supported by a cane, his eyes were bloated and his skin a shade of blue. She began to cry and he told her, 'Don't worry about me. I've lived twice.'

At a Hollywood partly he saw Olivia de Havilland, his

leading lady from so many classic films, including *Captain Blood* and *They Died With Their Boots On*. She was one woman who had really loved him, but had never enjoyed anything other than a purely platonic relationship. He slipped up behind her at the party and kissed her on the neck. She turned, but didn't recognize him for several moments.

While in Vancouver on 14 October 1959 at a Red Skelton Show, he fell ill. He told his young girlfriend, Beverley Aadland, that he would see a doctor, but instead he locked himself in the bedroom where he jabbed himself and took a few swigs of vodka.

That evening they went to a small party where the host, a Dr George Gould, examined him and told him he should lie down. But Errol spent the next two hours reminiscing to a spellbound audience. Finally he felt so ill he agreed to lie down.

'I shall return,' he announced, but before he could reach the bed he suffered a massive heart attack. The biggest Hollywood rogue of them all died in hospital. He was only fifty but the coroner stated that Flynn had the body of an old man.

2

Rampant Rogues

Right from its very beginnings, Hollywood could boast that it had the most beautiful girls in the world. Most of them were actresses. Some wanted to be actresses but came seeking fame and fortune and found themselves resorting to the oldest profession to make ends meet.

For any rampant rogue, Hollywood was a veritable stud farm.

'For any film star earning thousands who wanted a woman for a night or an hour without the ramifications of a romance and possible marriage, or even remarriage, money was never going to be the object,' Jesse Lasky Jnr once told me.

When Carole Lombard turned up on the set of *Twentieth Century* once day in 1934 to find that her co-star, John Barrymore, was not in attendance, she knew exactly where to find him. It was a rather undignified case of coitus interruptus for Barrymore when Carole stormed into a local brothel, extracted him and duly returned him to the set.

But not all the Hollywood studs needed, or wanted, to release their passions on women of ill repute. William Desmond Taylor, a director famous in the twenties for making films suitable for the family, was faithful to the very end – with

Mabel Normand, Mary Miles Minter, Mary's mother Charlotte Shelby *and* screenwriter Zelda Crosby.

They were all heartbroken when Taylor was murdered in his study on the night of 1 February 1922. The ensuing murder investigation revealed the scandalous life of a man who, because of the public outcry over the alleged rape and murder committed by Fatty Roscoe Arbuckle just a few months before, had vowed to clean up Hollywood. The Paramount executives certainly tried to clean up – the police arrive at Taylor's bungalow to find Paramount boss Adolph Zukor and Charles Eyton, general manager of Famous Players-Lasky, desperately trying to dispose of illegal booze and piles of papers. Mabel Normand was there too, searching for the love letter she'd written to Taylor, which police later found hidden in the pages of an erotic book, aptly titled *White Stains*.

Police also uncovered a collection of women's panties which Taylor kept as souvenirs, along with photographs of Taylor making love to a number of well-known actresses.

For Mary Miles Minter, the sweet, innocent, demure rival of Mary Pickford, it was the end of her screen career when an item of clothing was discovered among his souvenirs with the initials MMM embroidered on.

There was no knowing for sure just who *wasn't* involved with Taylor. It was claimed he was also into drugs, and Mabel Normand became implicated further when it was discovered that she was regularly sniffing cocaine. That was enough to bring a premature end to the brilliant comedienne's career.

Yet despite all the hanky-panky that came to light, and with a whole string of suspects that included his lovers and various shady characters – including the butler, who turned out to be his own brother – no one was ever brought to trial for his murder. It is, however, generally considered that the culprit was Charlotte Shelby who decided to shoot the rogue for stealing her little girl's innocence.

That lovable comic with the big boots, cane and bowler, Charles Chaplin, narrowly avoided the shotgun going off when he wed sixteen-year-old Mildred Harris in 1918. The public loved Charlie Chaplin. So had Edna Purviance, Josephine Dunn, Clare Sheridan, Pola Negri and Peggy Hopkins Joyce. But, according to Bernard Long, a one-time designer in the United Artists advertising department, 'Chaplin had a particular taste for young girls which got him into a lot of trouble.'

The world joined in unison to sing 'The Moon Shines Bright on Charlie Chaplin'. It beamed all over him the night he met blonde, blue-eyed Mildred at a beach party at Santa Monica. When she informed him some time later that she was pregnant, he did the decent thing and married her on 23 October 1918. She was sixteen. He was twenty-nine.

Two days after the wedding, rising mogul Louis B Mayer signed 'Mrs Charlie Chaplin' to a contract and starred her in *The Inferior Sex*. Chaplin was furious that Mayer should exploit his name and his wife.

Mildred almost died during the birth of their hideously deformed son. Mercifully, the child lived only three days. There was nothing left in the marriage to save it and soon after Chaplin moved out of the conjugal home. Chaplin may have loved to love, but he loved to talk as well, and he found Mildred was 'no mental heavyweight'.

Mildred brought a complaint of cruelty against her husband, who retaliated by charging infidelity. Who her extra-marital bedmate was he didn't say. He was enough of a gentleman not to reveal that Mildred was meeting with lesbian Russian star Ally Nazimova.

Mildred claimed that he was so tight with his money that he had scrimped on their son's funeral. Instead of hiring a hearse, she said, he had borrowed a car belonging to the Gish sisters. Like W C Fields, Chaplin's attitude to money was deeply affected by an impoverished childhood that left him with a lifelong fear of poverty. Hal Roach said, 'Charlie was one of the tightest guys I ever knew,' and King Vidor believed that Chaplin never could convince himself that he was a rich man who was able to enjoy extravagance.

They were divorced in 1920. Anyone would have thought he would have learned by his mistake. But four years later he was taking his second heavy-with-child child-bride down the aisle. She was Lilita McMurray.

When Chaplin first met her, she was a seven-year-old moppet playing in Kitty's Come-On Inn where her Spanish mother, Nana McMurray, worked as a waitress. Nana began to see her little girl's future taking shape as she served tea and cake to Chaplin who engaged the girl in a bit of pantomime.

He found the girl work as an extra and she graduated to walk-on parts. She appeared as an angel in *The Kid* in 1921, by which time she was thirteen, and followed it with *The Idle Class*, in which she played a maid. Nana McMurray was able to quit her job and set about planning her little Lilita's future – and, apparently, Chaplin's.

Lilita was raised to the rank of major star when Chaplin cast her in *The Gold Rush*. Her name was now change to Lita Grey. Press releases peppered the newspapers, announcing the arrival of a major new star as cameras began turning on *The Gold Rush*. Chaplin as director exposed miles of film on the dance-hall scene in which Lita tangoed. But something about her dancing dissatisfied him and for days he tried to capture a few magic moments on film.

According to Bernard Long who worked for United Artists, 'It's said that Chaplin was filming Lita dancing around the set when she suddenly grabbed her tummy and screamed. That's when Chaplin realized she was pregnant. And everyone else knew it too.'

Mrs McMurray, who was always standing in the side-lines, came over, calling upon all the Saints in Spanish, and fainted. Recovering miraculously quickly from the shocking news, she got on the phone to her brother-in-law, Edwin McMurray – a lawyer.

Uncle Ed was quickly on the scene, warning Chaplin that sex with an underage girl was statutory rape. This time Chaplin seemed intent on avoiding another shotgun wedding, and he offered Lita a 'dowry' of $20,000 plus assistance in finding a suitable young husband. But the whole McMurray clan wanted a wedding with *Chaplin* as the groom. Poor bothered and bewildered Charlie sought comfort in the arms of actress Marion Davies.

Davies was the mistress of newspaper tycoon William Randolph Hearst, who became a film producer for the sole purpose of creating the perfect star vehicles for Marion. He refused to marry her. He was already married and had no intention of getting a divorce. He was suspicious that Marion was carrying on with Chaplin and hired private detectives to spy on them. In an effort to keep a closer eye on them, he invited Chaplin to a party on his yacht. Director Thomas Ince came too, and died under mysterious circumstances. Hearst doctored reports of Ince's death so that the official verdict was that Ince died from 'acute indigestion'. But a careful examination of all that happened on the yacht (see *The Hollywood Murder Casebook*, Robson Books, 1987) points clearly to a cover-up by Hearst who, it was said, shot Ince, probably mistaking him for Chaplin.

To discredit this story Chaplin denied he was ever on board – his presence and affair with Marion Davies were key clues to the riddle. So Chaplin suddenly found a good enough reason to rush Lita Grey off to Mexico on 24 November 1924 for a quickie wedding. Lita's mom and Uncle Ed went too.

Just to make sure everyone knew about the 'secret' wedding, Hearst sent along one of his ace reporters to pursue the expectant bride and groom through the honeymoon. It's possible that Hearst ensured that other newspapers were tipped off too because Chaplin and the McMurrays arrived in Empalme in the state of Sonora to be greeted by a mob of news-hungry reporters. They reported that Chaplin looked 'grey' as he fought his way through, and failed to smile convincingly as he 'no commented' every pertinent question fired at him.

The wedding night was spent on a train bound for Los Angeles. Hearst's newshound stuck with the Chaplins all the way, and when Chaplin joined a group of close friends on the train, he was heard to say, 'Well boys, this is better than the penitentiary. But it won't last.'

In a more solemn moment that night, he said to Lita, 'You know, it would be easy if you'd just jump. We could end this whole situation if you'd just jump.'

When they arrived home, to Charlie's horror his mother-in-law moved in too. She insisted that Lita was too young to manage a household. He told Lita what to expect from their marriage. 'I don't intend to be a husband to you. You have your mother live with us because you can't live alone all the time in your condition.'

Possibly without Lita's knowledge, mother and Uncle Ed set about discovering just how much Chaplin was worth. They estimated he had assets worth $16,000,000.

Lita 'retired' from the screen and on 28 June 1925, gave birth to Charles Spencer Chaplin Jnr. Charlie Snr should have maintained some strict self-control. But just nine months later, on 30 March Lita gave birth to a second son, Sydney Earle Chaplin.

Chaplin began work on *The Circus*, a picture which for numerous reasons was one Chaplin preferred to forget. He didn't even mention it in his memoirs, and although originally released in 1928, he didn't allow it to be rereleased, as were most of his films, until 1969. His tribulations surrounding this film seem in the main to have been personal. He was miserable being married to Lita although according to her he 'was beginning to be very nice' around the time Sydney was born.

But things soon changed. Said Bernard Long, 'Chaplin needed a new leading lady for *The Circus*. I believe it was Lita who suggested a friend of hers, Merna Kennedy. Soon Chaplin was involved with Merna Kennedy, and that signalled the end of the marriage. Much has been made of Lita's relations interfering with the marriage, and I think to an extent that's true, but I don't believe Lita ever connived against him in any way. She was still so young and couldn't have really understood what was going on.'

One night Chaplin returned home, exhausted from the

day's filming of *The Circus*, and found the McMurrays raving it up at his expense. Chaplin exploded, there was an enormous row, and Lita stormed out with their two sons and, to Charlie's relief, the rest of the McMurray clan. Lita filed for divorce in 1927.

Uncle Ed sold a copy of the bill of divorcement to an unscrupulous publisher who produced a booklet outlining Lita's complaints for the whole world to read. It was a bestseller in which Lita, or more probably Uncle Ed, mixed fact with fiction, stating that Chaplin had seduced Lita; that he had forced her to marry him; that he had subjected her to 'cruel and inhumane treatment' to precipitate a divorce.

Part of this treatment, it was claimed by Lita's lawyers, was to force her to perform oral sex. The lawyers elucidated for those baffled by the term 'fellatio' by explaining that Lita objected to performing this 'abnormal, against nature, perverted, degenerate and indecent act'.

During the court hearings Lita recounted a number of conversations in which he attempted to 'undermine and corrupt her moral impulses', as her lawyers put it. She said that he suggested they engage the services of a particular girl so that they could all 'have some fun together'. When she refused to do as he wished he screamed, 'Just you wait. I'll blow my top one of these days, and I'll kill you.'

It all became very difficult to separate the lies from the truth. The divorce was a public humiliation for Chaplin who had undoubtedly been stupid enough to get an underage girl into trouble, but had then been manoeuvred by Lita's cunning and crafty family into a marriage and divorce.

Chaplin issued the following statement to the press:

I married Lita Grey because I loved her and, like many other foolish men, I loved her more when she wronged me, and I am afraid I still love her. I was stunned and ready for suicide that day when she told me that she didn't love me but that we must marry. Lita's mother often suggested to me that I marry Lita, and I said I

would love to if only we could have children. I thought I
was incapable of fatherhood. Her mother deliberately
and continuously put Lita in my path. She encouraged
our relations.

Years later Lita reflected on the marriage with less
bitterness, concluding that he was not really a cruel man but a
very insecure man which made him impossible to live with.
He had no real confidence in himself and once asked Lita,
'How could anybody love me? I'm not tall, dark and
handsome. Why would anybody love me?'

The trial seemed set to drag on until Lita threatened to
name in court five prominent actresses with whom Chaplin
had been intimately involved during their marriage. He
suddenly decided to agree on a cash settlement of $625,000
whereupon Lita agreed to change her complaint to a single
charge of cruelty – and Chaplin was free again.

He refrained from bedding girls who were under age, but he
still had an eye for the young ladies. He was forty-three and
white-haired when he met and fell in love with twenty-one-
year-old starlet, Paulette Goddard, a bleached-blonde divorcee
and a member of the Hal Roach stock company. She met
Chaplin just as she was about to invest her $500,000 alimony
in a film venture that he recognized as a pure phoney. He
stopped her in the nick of time and bought her contract from
Roach. She was now his own *ingénue* and he conceived *Modern
Times* as a vehicle for the two of them. Chaplin coached her
and had her grow out the blonde colouring so that she was a
brunette again. He began writing the script in 1932. A year
later they were secretly married while on a trip to the Orient.
The film was finally completed and premièred in 1936 when
they made their marriage public.

As she became a more established star working with other
leading men, and as Chaplin became more exacting, their
marriage ran aground. Chaplin was angered by her agent's
demands over billing of *The Great Dictator* in 1940. They
parted and were divorced in 1942, apparently without

bitterness. She went on to marry Burgess Meredith, and Chaplin became involved with Joan Barry. It was a disastrous liaison.

Barry, an aspiring actress, arrived in Hollywood in 1940. She took various odd jobs, including waitressing, and was invited to join a party of girls heading for Mexico for a huge bash. There she met United Artists agent Tim Durant who introduced her to Chaplin.

He was then fifty-four. She was twenty-two. In typical style, Chaplin screen-tested her (for *Shadow and Substance*, which was never made) and she became the leading lady in his life. Joan drank a great deal and was highly neurotic. Chaplin, seeing all the warning lights flashing, ended the affair, giving her money and paying her fare back to her home in New York.

Around this time Chaplin met and fell for Oona O'Neill, the daughter of playwright Eugene O'Neill. She was only seventeen.

Joan Barry, however, was obsessed with Chaplin, and returned to Hollywood a few months later, turning up at his home and brandishing a gun. According to Barry, he disarmed her and made love to her on a bearskin rug. Then he sent her on her way. She was picked up for vagrancy and turned up again at his home a few days later. The police were called and she was told to leave town. She didn't, and a few days later broke into his house. She was arrested and sentenced to thirty days' detention. She promptly announced that she was three months pregnant, naming Chaplin as the father.

Chaplin married Oona in June 1943 in Carpenteria in California, and, following the honeymoon, returned to Beverly Hills to find that Joan Barry had slapped him with a paternity suit. Instrumental in the case were the two battle-axes of the gossip columns, Hedda Hopper and Louella Parsons, who had decided that Chaplin had had his day and were all set to bring him down. Together their columns reached some 75,000,000 people and exerted a unbelievable influence over the public's attitudes.

Emphatically denying that he was the father, Chaplin

agreed to a blood test. It proved him innocent, but for reasons
that can only be attributed to America's growing animosity
towards him, the law rejected the blood test evidence. The FBI
was called in and Chaplin was indicted by a federal grand jury
on four counts under the Mann Act, which prohibited the
transportation of women (i.e., Miss Barry) from one state to
another for immoral purposes (i.e., getting laid).

Finally, in April 1944, Chaplin was acquitted on all counts.
But by that time his name had been well and truly blackened by
the press. He was considered by many to be a traitor and a
Communist, and they damned him for having never become an
American citizen while continuing to make a fortune there.

His troubles over Joan Barry returned two years later when
the paternity case was reopened and, despite all the evidence to
the contrary, he was legally found to be the father of Barry's
child and ordered to support the child.

The succession of scandals involving young women and his
so-called left wing politics led to America ostracizing him, and
upon finishing a tour of Europe, he was refused entry back into
America. He was condemned by the US Attorney-General as 'a
person of unsavoury character'.

As far as his politics went, he was never a Communist. But
neither was he a capitalist, and in the political climate of
America in the late forties and fifties, that meant being a
'pinko'.

As for his being a dirty old man, many, even people like Lita
Grey, look back on his dallyings with young girls as something
not so much seedy as, in some way, creative. Lita felt that he
was attracted to the virginal type as 'part of his creativity. He
wanted to see the girl awaken. He wanted to create a person.'

His last marriage, to Oona, was his most successful and
long-lasting. He said of her, 'I've been looking for somebody
like her all my life. If I'd found her before. I wouldn't have had
all the problems I've had in the past.'

In a sense, Chaplin was a purveyor of the 'casting couch'
technique, but a man who turned his own casting couch into a

legend was Mack Sennett. He began as an actor at the Biograph in 1908, and by the time he left them four years later he was an experienced director. He set up his own company, Keystone, which became the leading studio of slapstick comedy. Virtually every great screen comic of the era began with Sennett.

By all accounts, however, a much loved man he was not. In fact, hardly anybody had a good word to say about him, most finding him crude and vulgar. When anybody left his studio to work elsewhere he branded them as traitors.

Among his great discoveries – the Keystone Kops, Chaplin, Arbuckle – was the power of the casting couch. That must have kept him pretty busy when he introduced his famous Bathing Beauties, who became a hallmark of his films.

When Mabel Normand fell for him, nobody could really understand why. She was generally acknowledged as the most talented comedienne of the silent screen, but Sennett never allowed her to fully develop her talent at Keystone.

Her affair with Sennett lasted seven years, ending in 1915 when she came home one day and discovered a half-dressed Sennett with a completely naked Mae Busch. Mae was supposedly Mabel's best friend, and Mabel had brought her from New York to work in films. Sennett's amazing explanation of his compromising position was that he was merely discussing Mae's first role!

For her part, Mae's only reaction was to smash a vase over her 'best friend's' head. Mabel turned up an hour later, with blood pouring from a head wound, at the Arbuckles'. Two weeks later she tried to kill herself by jumping off Los Angeles Pier, and was dragged half dead from the Pacific.

She never fully recovered emotionally from Sennett's treachery, and her eventual downfall was brought about by cocaine addiction and her bizarre involvement with William Desmond Taylor.

For decades, talk of Hollywood orgies had filtered through to the outside world, but most people were careful not to let their rampant parties become public knowledge. However, a

Christmas party in 1940 held at Lionel Atwill's Pacific Palisades home proved a prime example of fun-loving frolics for film folk.

Lionel Atwill had been a gentlemanly veteran of the London stage before becoming a Broadway actor during the twenties. In the thirties he became a star of horror films such as *The Vampire Bat, Son of Frankenstein* and *Mark of the Vampire*. He also played featured roles in other films like *Captain Blood* and *The Three Musketeers*.

In 1939, following the break-up of his marriage, Atwill began staging the best orgies in town. Regulars there included director Joseph Von Sternberg and Eddie Goulding. Role-playing was a skill all guests had to be adept at, and all had to prove they were VD-free. There were twenty-six such guests at his 1940 Christmas party. Porno films were shown, and everyone had a high old time.

Nobody would have known about it if a pregnant sixteen-year-old girl called Sylvia, from Hibbing, Minnesota, hadn't revealed to her father, and then the police, that she had been a frequent visitor to the home of Lionel Atwill. Atwill was brought before a grand jury, charged with contributing to Sylvia's delinquency, at which the girl's friend and mentor, Virginia Lopez, a dress designer from Havana, testified that Atwill had shown two stag movies during the orgiastic Christmas celebrations. Atwill denied owning any such films. Virginia also testified that during a visit to Atwill's house she had seen Sylvia engaged in horse play with producer Eugene Frenke.

The jury found themselves impressed with Atwill's dignified manner and acquitted him, while Virginia Lopez found herself charged with corrupting the underage Sylvia. Lopez, it transpired, was a professional blackmailer who found young women ready to shake down men with money. When Lopez had found Sylvia, the girl was already pregnant, with no idea who the father was.

That should have been the end of that but a character called Carpenter, serving time in 1942, said he was prepared to spill the beans about the 1940 Christmas party in exchange for redemption. Carpenter, a two-bit actor, had been among the regulars at Atwill's home, and he was prepared to give the District Attorney the names of everyone who had been at the party as well as all the explicit details of what went on.

Atwill couldn't be charged for the same offence again, so this time the charge was perjury. Urged by his lawyer to tell the truth, Atwill admitted that he had rented a few blue movies to show to a house guest – a Royal Canadian Mounted Policeman. But, said Atwill, he hadn't seen the films himself. And, he emphasized, he had never behaved improperly with Sylvia.

The jury found him guilty of having perjured himself at the first trial. In fact, the jury were so unconvinced this time by Atwill that he was brought up on another charge, of perjuring himself before the 1942 jury as well as holding an orgy. This time Atwill admitted showing the pornographic films, and agreed to plead guilty to perjury if the DA dropped the orgy charge. Atwill was given a five-year probationary sentence.

Atwill now found himself unwanted by any of the studios – even though producers from those studios had been among his party guests. He applied for the probation to be terminated in the hope he might again find work. The judge chose to exonerate Atwill completely on the grounds that the 'person who caused this complaint to be made against Atwill was not actuated by a sincere desire to bring about justice'.

He managed to land roles in a few films, but his days were numbered. During the filming of a cheap serial in 1946, *Lost City of the Jungle*, he died from pneumonia. Many in Hollywood bowed their heads in shame to have rejected a man who had supplied some of the best fun in town.

Lionel Atwill was not the kind of man that Hollywood abhorred. What the establishment couldn't abide were the Twilight Men, as homosexuals came to be known in Hollywood. To be homosexual was damnable, and any actor who dared to come out of the closet, or who was discovered to be hiding in it, was swiftly dealt with by the studios, as happened to William Haines, one of MGM's most popular stars of the twenties. Audiences loved his screen image: charming, breezy, wisecracking and even arrogant. A graduate from the military academy in his home town of Staunton, Virginia, he won a 'New Faces' competition held by Samuel Goldwyn in 1922 and was put under contract. After Goldwyn merged with the Metro company, Haines was put into around six MGM films a year.

He was the first star at MGM to talk on film, in *Alias Jimmy Valentine* in 1928. But his career came to a sudden halt when Mayer fired him in 1933. The reason was because Haines had been arrested by the vice squad after being found at San Diego's YMCA with one of his many naval pick-ups.

Studio executives had already become aware of Haines's preference for men, especially men in uniform. Mayer had told Haines that he was to get married, preferably to Pola Negri with whom Mayer had linked Haines publicly in the press, in an attempt to stop the public outcry that would erupt if it became common knowledge that Haines was gay.

But Haines didn't want to marry anyone, least of all a woman. Besides, he had a lover, his stand-in Jimmy Shields. But Haines, in those pre-AIDS days, liked casual pick-ups. It was such a pick-up that led to his bust by the police and subsequent sacking by MGM. Mayer ensured that Haines was never again employed by any other studio. So Haines, and his lover, turned to a favourite pastime of theirs to make money – interior decorating. They lived happily ever after – or until 1973, when Haines died from cancer. Shortly after, Jimmy Shields took his own life. In those heady days of Hollywood, such men were outright rogues and dealt with as such.

Today society is more prepared to allow people to live their own lives. although there was still shock and horror when Rock Hudson's homosexuality became public when he was dying from AIDS. Not that it had been much of a secret. Everybody in the business knew the truth, but nobody ever talked. Not even the newspapers. Only when he was dying from the so-called Gay Plague did the public learn his long-kept secret. No, nobody could accuse Rock Hudson of being a rogue because of his homosexuality. What is unforgivable was his continual promiscuity with young men during the thirteen months he knew he had AIDS. His only consideration towards them while he was on his death bed was to have letters written to three men urging them to have a check-up.

Hudson didn't even bother letting his regular boyfriend, Marc Christian, know that he had AIDS. According to Christian, who sued Hudson's estate because of the anguish he had undergone knowing Hudson may have given him AIDS, they had had sex on more than a hundred and twenty occasions after Rock Hudson knew he had the virus.

Being gay was one thing. Molesting boys something else. There was definitely something wrong with William Tatem Tilden who, as a supreme tennis champion, came to Hollywood in the twenties to make several movies and play tennis with the likes of Chaplin, Navarro, Valentino, Tallulah Bankhead, Garbo and Flynn.

Probably at the urging of others, he was seen about town with several beautiful actresses. But when his dates decided they'd make the first move, they found him impossible to arouse. He was impotent and turned on neither by women nor men. How he got his kicks was discovered in 1946 when he was arrested by police who found him fondling the son of a prominent producer in a car.

Tilden was put away for eight months. Some time after his release he was caught again by police as he picked up a boy outside the child's school. He was sent back to prison and re-emerged into society friendless and broke. He died in 1953 from a heart attack. Today he is all but forgotten.

Nobody has forgotten, or forgiven, Roman Polanski. Nor are they likely to, least of all Samantha Gailey (though his friends have made allowances for his behaviour). In 1977 Samantha was forced drugs by Polanski who then raped her. She was just thirteen.

His friends have said that it was the scars of his childhood in Poland during the war – he was used as target practice by German soldiers – and the ritual slaughter of his wife Sharon Tate in 1969 which led him to commit such an act.

In a letter written by producer Robert Evans to Judge Rittenband during the hearings, Evans highlighted the suffering that had gone into Polanski's life. 'If ever a person is deserving of compassion, I think it is Roman,' he wrote.

Mia Farrow also wrote in Polanski's defence, calling him 'a brave and brilliant man', while producer Howard Koch said that Polanski was 'a man of tremendous integrity', and added, 'I'm sure the situation he finds himself in now is one of those things that could happen to any one of us.'

It was February 1977 when Roman Polanski persuaded the mother of thirteen-year-old Samantha to permit him to photograph the girl at her home. Polanski was a hugely successful director with films such as *Rosemary's Baby* and *Chinatown* to his credit. He was an important person in Hollywood, and he'd told Samantha's mother that the photos were for a French magazine, *Vogue Homme*.

A few weeks later, on 10 March, Polanski took the girl to Jack Nicholson's house where, he told her, he would introduce her to the star. Nicholson wasn't at home so Polanski helped himself to the champagne from the fridge. Samantha refused a drink at first – she had drunk champagne before and it had brought on violent asthmatic attacks. Polanski assured her she had drunk bad champagne and that this would be all right. She accepted it.

Then she drank another glassful. She began to feel ill, finding difficulty in breathing. 'When will Jack Nicholson be here?' she gasped.

'Come,' he said, taking her by the hand, 'jump in the hot tub. It will make you feel better.'

Refusing to strip, she insisted he bring her bikini which she had in her bag in the car. He brought it for her, returning to find her slumped on the sofa. 'I shouldn't have had that champagne,' she moaned.

He urged her to hurry and get into her bikini and climb in to the bath where he would take some more pictures of her. She was finding it harder to breathe and her head swam. He gave her tablets which he said would help. This 'man of tremendous integrity' had in fact given her Quaalude.

While she perched precariously on the edge of the bath, he began snapping pictures. He told her to remove her top. When she insisted on first calling her mother, he made the call instead and convinced the mother that the topless shots would be tasteful. She would have the final decision over whether they could be used, he assured her. Foolishly, the mother gave her permission to shoot the pictures in her absence.

By this time the drug Polanski had given Samantha was taking effect and she was becoming delirious. He wasted no time taking his own clothes off and climbed into the bath with her. He removed her bikini top and fondled her breasts. While she slipped in and out of consciousness, he pushed down her briefs. But when he began to touch her more intimately she managed to kick him away and then she fell out of the tub and on to the floor, mumbling, 'I'm sick. I want to go home.'

He led her into the bedroom where she fell asleep on the bed. When she came to Polanski had his head between her thighs. He was now high on drugs, and she was hardly able to stay awake. He began to force his penis into her mouth, causing her to gag.

He told her he wouldn't do that again if she let him have intercourse with her. She was crying and refused him. 'You want no more in mouth?' threatened the film director Mia Farrow called 'a brave and brilliant man'. 'Then you let me fuck you.'

She gave in. After having normal intercourse with her, he sodomized her, causing her to shriek in pain. 'Shut up,' said the man Robert Evans wrote was 'deserving of compassion', 'otherwise I give it to you in the mouth again.'

Then he heard someone enter the house. For a few minutes

he left the frightened, semi-conscious, trembling child, and discovered Anjelica Huston, daughter of John Huston and girlfriend of Nicholson. She demanded to know what he was doing in the house and told him to leave. Polanski promised to go when he'd finished. He returned to the bedroom and had intercourse with Samantha once again. When he'd finished he emerged from the bedroom, followed by Samantha who was dazed and frightened.

Later, Huston said, 'She seemed sullen to me, which I thought was a little rude.' *Sullen?* The girl had been *raped*.

Polanski drove her home, where she told her boyfriend what had happened. He didn't believe her but her sister overheard the conversation and informed their mother who in turn called the police. Polanski was indicted by a Los Angeles County grand jury of six felony counts; furnishing Quaaludes to a minor, child molesting, unlawful sexual intercourse, rape by use of drugs, oral copulation, and sodomy. He was in a situation which, according to Howard Koch, was 'one of those things that could happen to any one of us'.

His attorney managed to get the charges reduced to one of unlawful sexual intercourse in exchange for a plea of guilty. But before he could be sentenced, Polanski fled to France and has never since returned to America where he is now an outlaw.

Polanski's friends continue to campaign for the law to allow him to return to Hollywood. Samantha's lawyer, Larry Silver, said, 'Polanski misjudges public opinion. He seems to think that people in America would now think it is OK to sexually abuse a young girl. But in fact, with child sex abuse cases gaining more headlines, public opinion is opposed to him more than ever.'

Roman Polanski is one rogue too despicable to love.

Oddly, the one rogue nobody can find it in them to hate is the one who must have succeeded in setting records with the rampant feats he accomplished, and who can never be described as an admirable character. Errol Flynn took his sexuality, like his drug-taking and drinking, to excessive heights – and lows. He couldn't resist women, but he didn't seem to have too much regard for them either, and often just used them. During the filming of *Don Juan*, Flynn hired the services of two prostitutes who sat on the sidelines waiting for the day's filming to finish.

Flynn believed in sharing his pleasures, and invited the film's director, Vincent Sherman, to join him in his dressing room with the girls.

'Errol, I don't know how you can do it,' cried Sherman who knew that Flynn wasn't in tip-top health. 'You work all day here and then go to the dressing room with these women!'

'Oh, it's nothing,' replied Flynn. 'I just lie there reading the trade papers while they work on me.'

A cockney actor recalled for me one of Flynn's little parties.

I was in an Errol Flynn film back in the fifties. He invited the cast and crew on to his yacht for dinner, and we all thought, 'Whoa, there'll be lots of women.'

We arrived and there was this huge table laid out with food, but no women. We sat down and ate and wondered when the women were going to appear. By the time we finished eating, we were all a little disappointed. We'd been expecting an orgy but there wasn't a single woman on board that we could see.

With the meal over, we all had plenty of wine and whisky, and suddenly I realized there was somebody under the table where I sat. My trousers were being undone, and as I looked around I could see from all the boys' faces the same thing was happening to them. Flynn began laughing. He'd hidden the women under the table all the time, and he thought it was marvellously funny to see our faces as these girls serviced us under the table.

When Flynn had first gone to Hollywood he fell in love with French-born actress Lili Damita. He seems to have been faithful to her during the time they shared her bungalow at the famed hospice for the rich, the Garden of Allah.

Lili was a woman who fascinated Flynn. She had a wild temper, and there were always virile men at her door. But she seemed to prefer the presence of homosexuals. One night at a party at the Garden, she introduced Flynn to another actor. 'Fleen,' she said in her charming accent, 'meet David Neeven.'

Flynn and Niven made a point of avoiding each other as each assumed the other had to be gay. Niven never knew it, but he came close to the truth that day.

Flynn and Lili decided to get married, possibly because Jack Warner had put on the pressure, as in those days a scandal could wreck a career. The Flynns squabbled a good deal, but somehow their marriage had enough going for it to make it last seven years.

When Flynn's first starring role in *Captain Blood* turned him into an overnight star, Lili burst into tears. A studio executive said to Lili, 'Congratulations, he's a star.'

'I know,' wept Lili, 'that's why I'm crying. It's also the end of our marriage.'

The marriage actually managed to survive until 1942, resulting in a son, Sean. But by then Flynn's unquenchable thirst for every pleasure in life had taken a new twist – he enjoyed sex with men.

He began his homosexual experimentation with teenage boys. He had to travel to Mexico for this since he couldn't afford to allow these tendencies to be made known in Hollywood. Flynn wasn't strictly homosexual. He was bisexual ... or maybe just totally sexual. He also enjoyed underage girls.

In 1939 he met Tyrone Power who was also bisexual, and the two had a brief but intense affair. Flynn was also on the lookout for teenage boys in Hollywood circles, having grown tired of having to retreat to Mexico for his gay adventures.

Flynn was also an exhibitionist, and loved stripping down to his shorts aboard his yacht for passers-by to admire. Women who came by in water-taxis just for a look often found themselves invited aboard and then bedded. There were so many eager women that Flynn shared them with his crew and friends, awarding each of his men with a badge that carried the image of an erect penis and testicles. He called his crew the FFF – Flynn's Flying Fuckers.

After Lili walked out on Flynn, he set about building his mansion on Mulholland Highway. Flynn's obsession with sexual images was reflected in the design and the furniture. Chairs were loaded with sprung penises; a cocktail cabinet was opened by pressing the testicles of a painted bull above the bar; pornographic books were to be found among volumes of Dickens and Kipling.

It was only a matter or time before Flynn got himself into some sort of trouble, and in November 1942 he was charged with the statutory rape of two girls. Peggy Satterlee claimed she had been raped on board his yacht. Betty Hansen was supposedly raped on land. Despite all evidence to the contrary, the DA seemed determined to make an example of him, and Flynn had to call upon expert defence lawyer Jerry Geisler. Both girls came from dubious backgrounds and eventually Flynn was acquitted. It's also dubious that Flynn was entirely innocent, judging by his track record. That he raped the girls is highly unlikely; that he had sex with one or both with their consent would seem probable.

Work on Mulholland Farm continued, and a master bedroom was built with a two-way mirror directly above the bed. From the room above, Flynn watched his friends making love to whores. He sought new sexual heights. He would make love to women while simultaneously watching men engage in homosexual acts. He enjoyed watching lesbians making love. He still sought single conquests, both men and women.

While he was married to Nora Eddington, she lived in a special wing built just for her, allowed to live there only if she didn't object to his sexual activities with others. But she was unable to stand it and moved out. She did, however, still spend time with Flynn and they enjoyed many weekends together on his yacht – until she discovered his log detailing all of his amorous goings-on on board.

After their divorce, Flynn married Patrice Wymore. Nora befriended her and often stayed at the house to keep her company while Flynn was off doing God knows what with whom.

Even when Flynn was in Africa filming *The Roots of Heaven* he made sure he didn't go without. Said John Huston, 'I used to hear cats meowing at night but when I looked I never saw any cats anywhere. Not at night nor in the day. It turned out that the French doctor who was giving Errol drugs was also supplying him with girls. They would sneak into camp at night and signal by meowing. Then he'd let them into his hut. Each girl had been treated by the doctor to ensure they didn't pass on any venereal disease to Errol.'

In his final months, his constant companion was seventeen-year-old Beverly Aadland. It was because she was underage that he fled in 1958 to Vancouver, where he died.

3

Rebels

In 1950 a film called *The Men* introduced a young actor to the screen who was to send shock waves through the established echelons of Hollywood. His name was Marlon Brando, and his crimes against the establishment were to be rude to influential columnists, to fail to turn up at functions (and when he did turn up he wore T-shirt and jeans), and publicly to deplore Hollywood and its natives.

A new breed of rogue had been born. The Rebel.

Brando was no matinée idol heady with wine, or movie star who had more chemistry than talent. He'd studied acting with Stella Adler, a follower of Stanislavsky's principles, and with the Actors' Studio, bringing his 'method' acting to the New York stage as early as 1943. His film début prompted Richard Winnington to write that Brando's 'combination of style, depth and range comes like a blood transfusion into cinema acting'.

Through a succession of fine films, including *A Streetcar Named Desire, Viva Zapata!, Julius Caesar, The Wild One* and *On the Waterfront*, he was established firmly as one of the great actors of the fifties. But his method baffled a lot on his peers. Brando's co-star in *The Wild One*, Lee Marvin, who was never one of Hollywood's saints, told me:

> Brando would keep everyone waiting for twenty minutes.
> Everyone thought he was concentrating. But I knew he
> was having a sleep. It made him secure and everyone else
> insecure.
>
> I respected Brando as an actor. Actors like him have a
> system of playing through something, and, between us, I
> could tell that he wasn't finding that something. So
> half-way through a take I saw this cigarette butt on the
> ground, and I went over to it and kicked the cigarette out
> of the way. Brando said, 'Why, you sonofabitch,' and I
> said, 'Well, up yours too, pal,' and then he was suddenly
> giving me all of it, and I could do no wrong.

It was director Joseph L Mankiewicz who had given Brando
the chance to prove he was more than just a mumbling slob by
casting him as Mark Antony in *Julius Caesar*. He also gave
Brando his first light comedy role in the musical *Guys and
Dolls* opposite Frank Sinatra. Brando had never sung before,
but when he felt that Sinatra was singing in the wrong
manner, he said to Mankiewicz, 'He's supposed to sing with a
Bronx accent. He's supposed to clown it up. But he's singing
like a romantic lead. We can't have *two* romantic leads.'

'I agree with you,' said the director. 'What do you suggest I
do?'

'Tell him,' insisted Brando.

Mankiewicz smiled at the notion of telling Sinatra how to
sing, and said, '*You* tell him.'

Brando was furious and said, 'I'm never going to work with
Mankiewicz again.'

In 1955, the year of *Guys and Dolls*, and again in 1958,
Brando was voted among the top ten box-office stars. But his
finest years found him in some competition with another actor
who, like Brando, refused to conform. Comparisons between
them became commonplace, but unlike Brando, this other

rebel was not so aggressive either on screen or off it. He was Montgomery Clift.

Clift came from a hugely successful New York stage background. His films were relatively few and he felt confident enough to turn down a good many more films than a hungrier actor might have felt was healthy. His nonconformity was not just limited to the roles he chose or to his moody persona but also to his sexuality. As a leading man in films he was expected to be nothing other than purely masculine. But he was a bisexual, and his sexuality was something that coloured his life to a great extent and, along with a chronic alcohol problem, contributed to his decline.

The reason for this, if only in part, was because Clift had been brought up in an era where homosexuality was considered a form of mental illness. For an actor, admission of homosexuality was tantamount to professional suicide, so it was necessary for Clift to hide the fact that he fell in love with men. It helped enormously that he also happened to enjoy affairs with women, and that when he was acting on stage, his sexual proclivities were not such a problem as he was less in the public eye. In 1940 he fell for an actor who was his lover for two years before joining the navy in 1942.

To gain further training Clift joined the Actors' Studio and there met Marlon Brando. Both actors came to epitomize 'the Method'. They never, however, became hard and fast friends and there was an unspoken rivalry between them. Monty thought Brando was 'too clownish and a slob'. Brando thought Clift too serious and intense.

By the time Clift had made his screen début in Howard Hawks's epic western, *Red River* (1948), he was drinking heavily and trying to conceal it, as he did his sexuality. It was a combination that destroyed his ability to cope with life, and he sought psychiatric help in 1950. Perhaps feeling somehow more secure in the company of a female therapist, he chose Dr Ruth Fox, who specialized in treating alcoholics. She persuaded him to join AA, and for a while he attended their weekly meetings. But when Clift confided in her about his homosexual tendencies, she referred him to a colleague whom she felt could help him infinitely more than she could. This was Dr William Silverberg who, unlike many of his colleagues of the day, did not look upon alcoholism as a form of weakness. More than that, *he* was a homosexual.

Silverberg became something of a hero to Clift, but analysis didn't help. Clift's drinking increased and his moods became more manic. He became hostile to his friends, and, as though trying to cure himself of his homosexual nature, he began pursuing women more vigorously than ever. He suffered from insomnia and was taking barbiturates. He was desperate to understand his sexuality, and afraid of becoming *totally* homosexual. He was a man in torment who finally decided that he was what he *did*, and not what anyone said he was.

Despite his personal trauma, his professionalism would never have been in question – if it hadn't been for the drink and drugs. Prior to filming *I Confess* in 1953, he prepared for his role as a priest by spending a week at a monastery just outside Quebec. He attended Mass every morning at four o'clock and was moved by the solemn dignity of the services. He refrained from taking any alcohol or drugs, but when he returned to Hollywood to commence filming, he began drinking again and was picked up by the police for drunken driving. And when the film's director, Alfred Hitchcock, threw a party at his house, Clift became so drunk that his co-star Karl Malden carried him out in his arms.

While filming *From Here to Eternity* Clift's behaviour grew more bizarre and temperamental. He complained that Burt Lancaster was getting top billing. 'He doesn't deserve to,' Clift ranted. 'He is a terrible actor, nothing but a big bag of wind, the most unctuous man I've ever met.'

He was in some respects schizophrenic. One moment he would radiate class and talk about acting with insight and intelligence. Then he would go and piss in the gutter. While he disliked Lancaster, he was fond of Frank Sinatra, and, according to Patricia Bosworth's excellent biography *Montgomery Clift*, even talked Sinatra out of committing suicide over his rejection by Ava Gardner.

Sinatra and Clift stayed close friends until one night, sometime after filming had been completed, Sinatra watched in repulsion as Clift made homosexual overtures to a guest at the party Sinatra was hosting, and had his bodyguards throw Clift out.

Deborah Kerr, who was in the film, told me, 'Monty was deeply immersed in his role. You couldn't get him to talk about anything else. And I only had one scene with him. But what I did notice about him was how much he wanted to love women. But instead he was attracted to men, and he crucified himself for it.'

Donna Reed, who had a number of scenes with Clift, said, 'When Monty was sober he was a wonderful, sweet, charming man. But when he drank he lost himself somehow.'

By 1953 the name of James Dean was being bandied about in theatre circles. Clift was told by director Elia Kazan that Dean idolized him and that although he liked Brando as well, he was more affected by Clift.

Dean was another rebel, no doubt modelling himself on his two idols. In Kazan's words, he was 'a punk and a helluva talent. He likes racing cars, waitresses – and waiters.'

He began phoning both Clift and Brando; Clift tried to discourage Dean, who began signing his letters 'James (Brando-Clift) Dean'.

His first film was *East of Eden*, which both Brando and Clift had turned down. Dean proved to be generally rude and disruptive to his fellow actors, and spent much of his free time in his dressing room, refusing to speak to anyone unless it directly concerned the film.

He had moved in with an older man, TV director Roger Brackett. The story that the fan magazines put out was that Dean and Brackett had a father-son relationship; the gossips suggested that if this was so, it was incestuous.

For Clift, Dean's arrival in Hollywood was a setback in his own film career. After *From Here to Eternity*, his choice of films often left much to be desired. He was constantly being compared to Brando, and vice-versa, which outraged him, and now Jimmy Dean was being hailed as the new Clift *and* the new Brando. But worst of all were the comparisons being made between Monty Clift and Jekyll and Hyde.

For years he had been close friends with Kevin McCarthy and his wife. But as Monty's physical and mental state were gradually ravaged by drink and drugs, even the McCarthys barred him from their home. Under the influence Clift was transformed from an articulate and relaxed friend into a repugnant oaf. Many of his other friends also disowned him.

One close friend who remained loyal to him was Jack Larson who played Jimmy Olsen in the TV series *Superman*. He was concerned that Clift's continuing sessions with Silverberg were making him worse, and he tried to get Silverberg to commit Clift to Silver Hill Sanatorium for a hopeful cure. Silverberg refused.

Throughout 1955 Clift didn't work at all. Dean, meanwhile, made *Rebel Without a Cause*, an exploitive title for a young actor who kicked against the pricks. During filming, he took to frequenting a Hollywood bar popular with the S & M crowd. A bondage freak himself, he would get high on dope and then let his sadistic friends use his chest as an ashtray.

He was also into quickie sex and wasn't too particular who he went with. Subsequently, he was often seen scratching at his groin on the set, and, guessing the nature of his problem, director Nicholas Ray marched him off to the nearest chemist for a healthy dose of crabocide.

In the Warners studio, he spat on the portraits of Bogart, Cagney and Muni, and he further proved his contempt for convention by throwing his steak out of the window at an important Hollywood dinner party. On the rare occasions when he consented to do interviews, he usually sat silent and still, staring stone-faced at baffled journalists.

Following the completion of *Rebel Without a Cause*, Warners put him straight to work on his third movie, *Giant*, an epic directed by George Stevens and featuring a stellar line-up including Eliabeth Taylor, Rock Hudson, Sal Mineo and Carroll Baker. The filming included several weeks on location in Texas. Local ranchers and townsfolk would gather about the set hoping to catch a glimpse of the stars. Jimmy Dean gave them more than they bargained for. He unzipped his fly and peed before their very eyes.

Stevens was one of the most meticulous of film directors and any actor working with him could expect a gruelling time. Dean made no secret of his hatred for his director, often arguing violently and calling Stevens every name under the hot Texan sun.

On 29 September 1955, with just a few days of filming to go, Dean turned up at a gay party at Malibu which culminated in a bitchy foray between Dean and a former male lover who accused him of dating women purely for publicity.

The next day Dean leapt into his brand-new Porsche. He had been forbidden to drive throughout filming by Warners because of the reckless speeds he drove at. Even though Stevens still needed Dean for a couple more shots, the young punk put his foot down and tore along Highway 66 at 85 miles an hour, heading for a sports car race at Salinas.

En route he raced and collided with another car. An ambulance gave him his last race to Paso Robles Hospital. He was declared DOA. His death was suddenly the birth of a whole new cult. *Rebel Without a Cause* had not yet been released, but suddenly every teenager made Dean their idol.

His neck had been broken and his chest smashed up. During the coroner's examination, he noted the 'constellation of keratoid scars' on the broken chest: mementoes of the time he was known as the Human Ashtray.

His death at the age of twenty-four made him an instant legend. Years later Elia Kazan said, 'What I disliked was the Dean legend. He was the glorification of hatred and sickness. When he got success he was victimized by it. He was a hero to the people who saw him only as a little waif, when actually he was a pudding of hatred.'

At the time of Dean's death Monty Clift was in New York with a girlfriend, black jazz singer Libby Holman. Most mornings she woke him with coffee and the newspapers. One morning she said, 'Isn't it terrible what happened to Jimmy Dean?'

'What happened?' asked Clift.

'He was killed on Highway 66. He was driving his silver Porsche. His neck was broken. His chest crushed when it smashed into the steering wheel.'

Clift threw up across the sheets. Dean's death had a profound effect on him – maybe he felt it to be a premonition.

In 1956 Clift starred with Elizabeth Taylor in the MGM civil war spectacle *Raintree County*. He had worked with Elizabeth in the 1951 picture *A Place in the Sun* and they had remained close friends. But there were problems.

Lee Marvin, who had a good supporting role in the film, told me, 'The big problem I had with Monty Clift was that he wouldn't look me in the eye. I mean, shit, I got to know what he's thinking, right? I got to react to him. But all he ever looked at was my forehead. I wouldn't have minded if I'd had a bump on my head, a cross on it or a bullet through it. I could understand that kind of fascination with my forehead. I tell ya, it threw me having those tormented eyes of Clift staring just above me.'

'I had to warn Monty about his drinking because he'd been causing trouble,' MGM's then chief of production, Dore Schary said to me. 'Even Elizabeth Taylor was upset by his behaviour but she loved him and didn't complain. Monty promised me that I had nothing to worry about. But I *was* worried, and somehow I had inside of me this feeling that something was going to happen. So I took out an insurance policy against a possible breakdown in the production. It had never been done before, but I had this premonition, and of course it proved true.'

While on his way to Elizabeth Taylor's for a dinner party, Clift crashed his car. He was terribly mangled and it was a miracle that he survived. It took half an hour for Rock Hudson and a doctor to pull him from the wreck. He was rushed to hospital with cerebral concussion and a smashed-up face.

Incredibly, Clift returned to the film several weeks later, but with his face disfigured and virtually immobile down one side. Throughout the rest of the filming, director Edward Dmytryk shot only Clift's good side – his right side – as far as possible.

'We did consider replacing Monty, but we had already shot half the movie,' said Dore Schary. 'We talked to Elizabeth, to Monty's doctor and to Monty, and we all decided that it would kill Monty if we took him off the picture. But it was Monty himself who made the final decision. He wanted to finish the film. I guess he felt he had to.'

But more than just physical damage had been incurred. Clift's insomnia increased, and when he did sleep he had nightmares. Twice he was found sleep-walking naked in the streets and had to be escorted back by police. He began experimenting with different drugs and drank excessively. He was so drunk one day that Dmytryk ordered him home, at which Clift kicked a tree in fury and broke a toe.

Even Brando became so concerned over Clift's drinking that he went to see him to try to persuade him to join AA. 'If you're afraid to go alone,' said Brando, 'I'll go with you. I'll help you dry out.'

Clift insisted he didn't have a drinking problem and Brando left believing Clift was 'a lost cause'.

The following year Brando and Clift were just two of an array of stars in the big-scale war film *The Young Lions*, but did not appear together. However, they did observe each other's work. Clift said, 'Marlon is sloppy – he's using about one-tenth of his talent.'

Maybe Brando agreed with Clift; in any case, sensing he had more to offer than an actor's tools, he decided to take his destiny into his own hands and he set about producing *One-Eyed Jacks*, a western, in 1960. For a while Sam Peckinpah worked with Brando on the script.

Said Peckinpah, 'Very strange man, Marlon. Always doing a number about his screen image, about how audiences would not accept him as a thief, how audiences would only accept him as a fallen sinner – someone they could love.'

Brando brought Stanley Kubrick into the project as the film's director and together they worked on the script for several months. Then Brando fired Kubrick and directed the film himself.

His next film was *Mutiny on the Bounty*. MGM were prepared to make the film as a star vehicle for him and originally offered him the role of Captain Bligh. But it was the part of Fletcher Christian that fascinated Brando, and he announced that he would play the part if the script was rewritten to his specifications. MGM agreed. They didn't even have a director at this point – just a star name. After wearing out writers, the script was completed, not entirely to Brando's satisfaction, but he told producer Aaron Rosenberg, 'If this is what you want, this is what you'll get. I'll just do anything I'm told.' Famous last words.

Carol Reed was chosen to direct, and he chose Trevor Howard to portray Bligh. The cast and crew set off for Tahiti. Friction arose between Reed and Brando who wanted to play Christian as a fop. Reed delayed filming his scenes in the hope that Brando might change his mind, but finally he gave up and quit. Lewis Milestone took over the helm, and he too found Brando impossible to direct. Even the cameraman ignored Milstone's command of 'Roll 'em' when Brando was talking to him. Milestone discovered that he didn't even have to yell 'Cut' because Brando would give the signal himself for the cameras to stop turning.

'I knew we were going to have a stormy passage right away,' said Milestone. 'I like to get on with things, but Brando likes to discuss every scene, every line for hours. I felt enough time had been wasted, but time didn't seem to mean anything to Brando. After a lot of bad feeling, the next thing I knew was Rosenberg, the producer, was on the set every day and Brando was arguing about every scene with *him* instead of me. When eventually the arguments were over, I'd be told Brando was ready for the cameras. It was a terrible way to make a picture.'

There was no love lost either between Brando and Trevor Howard, one of legend's great hellraisers. One day Howard came on the set and Brando was down the beach talking to a pretty girl. The assistant director called Brando who ignored him. Brando was called twice more before he returned, at which point Howard strode off in a rage.

Trevor Howard told me:

As an actor Brando is a great politician, but because of that he is destructive to those he works with. He was constantly demanding rewrites, even on the set, so you never knew where you were at any time. All the constant changing did was to make the next scene you were doing contradict the one you did yesterday, so all that had to be changed.

No, I didn't like Brando. I didn't hate him either. I think he is to be pitied because all he does is make enemies for himself. So he never makes friends. He didn't have a friend on Tahiti – except for the girl he played his love scene with.

I don't honestly know why he agreed to do the film, except that all he wanted was a fifteen-minute death scene.

The death scene was filmed back in Hollywood at the MGM studios. By then Milestone had had enough and quit. George Seaton directed the scene upon condition that Brando behaved. Brando did, and even welcomed Seaton's suggestions, such as the fact that a man who is dying of severe burns, as Christian does in the scene, shivers as though freezing. Brando had lumps of ice put under the blanket that covered him, and consequently his shivering is frighteningly realistic.

Stories emanating from the making of the film had producers becoming wary of Brando. The joy of acting left him. 'Acting is an empty and useless profession,' he said.

His private life was no more settled. From 1957 to 1959 he was married to Anna Kashfi and then to Movita Castenada from 1960 to 1961. He never married Tarita, his leading lady in *Mutiny on the Bounty*, but she did give him two children.

Monty Clift, in 1960, was faring better than Brando. He worked with Marilyn Monroe and Clark Gable in John Huston's monumental *The Misfits*. Monty recognized the trauma of drug addiction that Monroe suffered, both of them relying heavily on barbiturates to make them sleep.

At that time John Huston found little to complain of in Clift, but Clark Gable, who recognized that Monty was a gifted actor, had his patience stretched, as on one occasion John Huston told me about:

> Clark had a bad back – arthritis – and in one scene they are driving through the crowd going to the rodeo. Well, Monty kept punching Clark in the arm out of sheer exuberance. Clark kept saying, 'Please, stop', but Monty just kept hammering away and Clark said, 'For God's sake, Monty, take it easy.'
>
> When Clark took off his shirt he had black-and-blue bruises over his shoulders and arm. But Monty hit him again and Clark turned on him and said, 'I'm going to hang one on you, you little bastard, if you do that again.' Monty burst into tears and Clark looked at me and said, 'What the fuck is the world coming to?'

When Huston began his next project, *Freud*, he was enthusiastic to have Clift play the title role. But in the space of little more than a year he found that Clift had 'deteriorated to a shocking degree':

> Monty was supposed to be on the wagon and I certainly didn't see him drinking, until I discovered that every time he passed the bar he'd pick up any bottle that was on the bar and drink it. I knew also that he was on drugs. Because he'd been seeing psychiatrists since 1950 he fancied he was an expert on Freud and wanted to sit in on all our discussions. He kept interrupting and eventually I

told him he couldn't sit in on our discussions any more and I explained why. He stood outside the door and cried and then went and drank until he was out cold.

I realize now that I should have fired him right then but I thought at the time that when we got him on the set he would be OK. I was wrong. He kept trying to rewrite the script and would produce pages which he scrawled on so badly you couldn't read it, and neither could he. He also had difficulty remembering his lines, and eventually I had to write his lines on boards, on bottles, on door frames – anything he had to pass by or pick up.

There are stories of cruelty heaped upon Clift by Huston during the making of *Freud*, and when weighing up one person's story against another's you start wondering just who was the worse rogue. Susannah York was a young up-and-coming leading lady who had a major part in the film. She told me that she actually attacked Huston and hit him because of his treatment of Monty:

I sort of pummelled him on the chest, that was all. I used to get so angry on the set that one day I just blew my top and hit John Huston. Unfortunately, we didn't have a very happy working relationship. I didn't like the way he kept attacking Montgomery Clift. I loved Monty. I would do anything for him. We were intimate with each other – not in a romantic way but in terms of our working relationship. We would work together late into the night to get a scene right between us. And when Huston attacked Monty, not physically but verbally, I couldn't take it. Monty wasn't weak. He was strong and took it all from Huston in a strong way. It's just that *I* couldn't take it. Perhaps because I was so new to it all and naive.

After interviewing Susannah (this was back in 1980 on the set of *The Awakening*), I had the good fortune to meet and interview John Huston and I challenged him on Susannah's story. He had a different tale to tell.

Susannah York was very talented but spoiled. She was young and ignorant – let's say *uninformed*. Monty influenced her. He collected a group of protective converts, and he had this knack of making even the most reasonable request look like persecution. He converted Susannah and a few other female members of the company, and they were all aghast at the so-called brutal manner I treated Monty.

Monty influenced Susannah and she became convinced that she was entitled to scientific opinions regarding a subject she knew nothing about. So she and Monty would stay up all night rewriting their scenes, which they presented to me each morning.

Now, all this time I held my temper, even when he turned on the tears which he could do, playing skilfully on his little-boy manner which elicited great sympathy from the women. But as time went on the situation just got worse and costs started to escalate. I exercised all the patience I could muster, trying every trick I knew of to get a performance out of Monty.

Nothing worked. I finally decided it was time to get tough. I went to his dressing room and slammed the door behind me so hard the mirror broke. He looked up at me and I stared hard at him. I wanted him to feel my anger. He asked, 'Are you going to kill me?' I said, 'I'm seriously considering it.'

It was a tactic. I've read accounts of that incident in which I was supposed to have smashed everything up in his room. There's a story also of how I supposedly made him do take after take of a scene in which he slides down a rope until he was rope-burned so badly he had blood pouring from his hands. What really happened was that he had to climb a length of rope which had mattresses underneath it so that at the end of each take he could simply drop to the ground in safety. But for some reason each time I yelled 'Cut' he slid down the rope, holding very tightly, causing him severe rope burns. I don't understand it. Maybe he was desensitized by drugs.

No, I was never cruel to Monty. He was just *non compos mentis* most of the time and there were times when you could be forgiven for forgetting that he was a woefully sick man.

The on-set problems of *Freud* led to Clift suing Universal, claiming they hadn't paid him all of his $200,000 fee, and they counter-sued for nearly $700,000. Monty won, but the battle raged on until 1963, by which time no producer wanted to touch him. He was a shambles. He went cruising for boys and had numerous homosexual encounters, usually with complete strangers. He began hanging out at a seedy bar where transvestites, gay guys in leather jackets, and even butch lesbians, would lay him across a table and then crawl all over him.

It was Elizabeth Taylor who came to his rescue in 1964, trying desperately to get him working again. She wanted to make *Reflections in a Golden Eye* with him playing the latent homosexual army officer, and Taylor as his wife. Initially, Richard Burton was to direct, but he pulled out of the project and Taylor persuaded John Huston to do it. But producer Ray Stark couldn't get Clift insured to do the film, so Liz Taylor very generously agreed to pay the insurance herself. By mid-1965 work on the film had still not begun. There was one hold-up after another and all the time Clift became more and more frail.

Eventually a firm offer came from a European producer for a low-budget spy film, *The Defector*, shot in Munich in March and April of 1966. It was far from being his best film. In July word came that *Reflections in a Golden Eye* would begin filming in August. But on 22 July he died in bed from 'occlusive coronary artery disease'. He was just forty-five but looked twenty years older.

Reflections in a Golden Eye went ahead, with Clift's role being taken, ironically, by Marlon Brando. He had outlived both James Dean and Montgomery Clift but his film career was floundering. His films throughout the sixties were poorly received in America. Only in Britain was *Reflections* admired. In 1972 Hollywood suddenly sat up and took notice of him again when he had two consecutive hits, *Last Tango in Paris* and *The Godfather*, for which he won the Oscar for Best Actor. He displayed his contempt for Hollywood at the awards ceremony by refusing to accept the gold statuette and sending an Indian girl in his stead to protest at the way the movie industry had treated the Red Man. Marlon may have got involved in a noble cause, but it got a lot of people's backs up in the business.

In more recent years he has shown how he despises the movie industry by making only rare fleeting appearances. A storm erupted when he was payed a reputed £2,250,000 for what amounted to a cameo appearance in *Superman the Movie* in 1979. But as far as producer Ilya Salkind was concerned, it was money well spent. Before Brando was hired, no major stars wanted to touch the project, including Paul Newman who had the choice of playing either Jor-El or Superman.

'The moment we got Brando,' Salkind told me, 'everything started moving really fast. We got Gene Hackman the next day practically because just about every actor wants to play opposite Brando.'

Not *every* actor. According to Patrick Newell, Trevor Howard agreed to do the film only if he didn't have to work with Brando. Although Howard didn't actually have to come face to face with Brando, they had to share the same set. Harry Andrews, who was also in their scenes, told me, 'Trevor was quite sickened by the sum Brando was being paid, especially as Brando couldn't seem to remember his lines and had to read his dialogue off boards.'

Possibly because Brando prefers to be thought of as a man of the people, he tended to snub the other actors as well as the producers and director in favour of the company of the crew. One of the *Superman* crew members told me, 'During a party on the set, Marlon said to me, "Is there any more gin?" I said, "I believe there's some over in the producer's office. Come on over and we'll get some."

'He said, "Oh no. I'll stay here. I don't like producers or directors. Give me the technicians any time." '

Now extremely overweight and looking older than his sixty-five years, Brando spurns most film offers, although he appeared in *The Freshman* in 1989 and promptly denounced it to the world before it was even in the can. '*The Freshman* is going to be a flop,' he announced. 'It's horrible. After this, I'm retiring. I'm so fed-up. This picture, except for the Canadian crew, was an extremely unpleasant experience.'

He made these astonishing remarks when he called for a meeting with the *Toronto Globe and Mail*, much to the surprise of everyone. He told them, 'When you're exploded into the orbit of fame, if you're not careful you tend to believe your own publicity and then you really invite disaster.'

There have been others who have tried to emulate Marlon Brando. A few, like James Dean and Montgomery Clift, were his direct contemporaries. Those who tried to match his mood and magnificence have failed. He is the first and, outliving Dean and Clift, the last of the great Hollywood rebels.

4

Hellraisers

At some point during the fifties the press coined a phrase, not entirely new but then fashionable, for any actor who emulated the lifestyle of Errol Flynn, if only in part. All they had to do was live life through an alcoholic haze and generally raise hell – hence the term 'Hellraiser'.

One man had it down to a fine art – Lee Marvin. For him raising hell meant having a wonderful time. And he did. It also meant living a certain philosophy. As Lee Marvin put it to me once, 'Take no shit from anybody.' And he meant *anybody*.

He learned that lesson from his hero, Humphrey Bogart, who was one of the great hellraisers before anyone thought of the term. Bogie was the kind of hellraiser who lived at one end of the scale. As Marvin told me, 'Bogie did it Bogie's way.' Whereas Flynn was at the other end of the scale, for, despite his external charm, he really seemed to care little about anybody's well-being – possibly because he cared nothing for his own.

Bogie, however, *cared*. He cared enough about his loathsome, drunken and violent third wife, Mayo Methot, not to leave her until he knew she had gone to the furthest extremes to try and cure herself of the alcoholism that threatened to ruin both their lives. Only when it became totally apparent that she would never reform and was bent on self-destruction for both of them did he leave her for the younger and more stable Lauren Bacall.

'When Bogie acted tough with people,' said Marvin, 'that's all he was doing – *acting*. He was never unpleasant with people. But he knew how to put the fear of God into producers and directors – I learned from this very quickly while playing a small role in *The Caine Mutiny* [in which Bogart starred as Captain Queeg].' Marvin continued:

We were in Hawaii for two weeks before Bogie arrived. We were all ready on the ship – Eddie Dmytrik the director and Stanley Kramer the producer – when Bogart arrived.

They began filming and there must have been something wrong because Bogie just sort of walked straight through the shot, so Eddie says, 'Bogie, you walked right through that shot.'

Bogie said, 'Well, you can shoot it again, can't you?'

Then Eddie said, 'You'll be in the next shot so if you'll slip into your rags we'll ...'

'Where's my dressing room?' asked Bogie, interrupting.

'Well, this is the navy,' said Kramer. 'We don't have any dressing rooms.'

'Well, I'm not in the navy,' said Bogart, and he walked through the ship, up and down. And I'm there. I want to see this. Bogie says, 'Whose room is this?'

I said, 'This is the Captain's quarters.'

'I'll take this room,' said Bogie.

So then he's doing a scene and he's wearing a khaki shirt which has a sweaty spot on it. They want to take another shot and Bogart says, 'Let me have a clean shirt, please.'

'That's the only one we have here,' they said.

'Okay,' he said. 'I'm going to catch a boat back to the

mainland and I'll be in my hotel where you can call me when you've got a clean shirt for me.'

And I'm watching all this and thinking, 'Jeez, have I got a lot to learn.'

He wasn't just playing at being the *star*. He was in a position to control the way the work came out and he was going to exercise it. And he was right. He'd say, 'OK, let's get on with it. We'll have a drink at my house later but don't let's fuck around here.'

Lee may have found all that a valuable lesson, but there were times when it seemed Marvin just hadn't learned at all. Stories of his drinking and coming to work drunk were many. When he made *The Dirty Dozen* in 1967, he failed to turn up to film the final scene, when he and Charles Bronson drive a huge weapons carrier across a bridge. Producer Ken Hyman went in search for him and found him in a bar in Belgravia 'as drunk as a skunk'. Hyman hustled him into a car and, having come prepared with a flask, poured coffee into him as they drove to the studio.

All the way back Marvin was singing and joking. When they arrived on the set he almost fell out of the car. Charlie Bronson was furious and threatened to kill Marvin. Hyman got between the two of them, begging, 'Don't hit him, Charlie.'

Marvin climbed into the weapons carrier and began driving it as director Robert Aldrich called, 'Action!' The scene went perfectly and watching the film you might never suspect that Lee was in fact very drunk.

Unlike a good many tough guys who made it big in movies, Marvin didn't come from a particularly tough background. He was born in New York to an advertising executive and his journalist wife. They lived in Madison Avenue and young Lee wasn't deprived of anything. However, even at kindergarten his rebellious streak was showing and at the age of five or six he was playing truant. He had something of a Huckleberry Finn spirit, wanting to run away to sea. So at the age of sixteen he enlisted in the Marines. He saw action in the Pacific, was wounded and was awarded the Purple Heart, and always remained very proud of his Marine background.

He studied acting under the GI Bill and after touring in summer stock he began landing parts in television as heavies.

He told me:

I played a couple of hundred sons-of-bitches on TV and was making some good money from it so I could afford to buy as much booze as I wanted. I don't know if I was drinking really heavy then, but I was young and I wasn't Number One yet, or even Number Two, so you want to do anything and everything. It becomes like a drive because you're afraid of not making it, so, yeah, I drank.

At first I drank beer because I couldn't afford to drink anything else, but then it became Martinis. And after the third glass I'd become a little boisterous, aggressive even. Another actor would walk in and I'd say, 'What an asshole!' and the barman would say, 'Enough, out.' And that would be one more bar we couldn't go back to.

The thing that made Lee Marvin such a perfect rogue is that, despite all the stories of his being drunk on the set and causing producers to have palpitations, there is probably no single director or actor who worked with him who didn't think the world of him. Maybe it has something to do with the curious outlook he had on life.

Actor Ed Lauter, who worked with Marvin and knew him well, told me:

There's this story bout Lee. He's out in the desert making *The Professionals* with Burt Lancaster, Robert Ryan and director Richard Brooks. They've stopped filming and they're standing on a rock and Lee says, 'Burt, you were in the army. What rank were you?'

Burt says, 'Private First Class.'

'Robert, you were in the Marines. What were you?'

Robert Ryan says, 'Private First Class.'

'Richard, Marines?'

'Private First Class.'

So there are all these millionaires standing on the rock and Lee says, 'I wonder what all those fucking generals are doing now?'

When one hellraiser comes face to face with another, everyone battens down the hatches and prepares for all hell to break loose. And that's what the good citizens of Oroville in California did when Lee Marvin teamed up with Richard Burton to film *The Klansman* in 1974. If there was anyone in the world who could match Marvin drink for drink it was Richard Burton.

As the two hellraisers met for the first time for the benefit of the world's press, they exchanged jokes.

'I guess you know I get top billing in this,' said Marvin.

'Yes,' replied Burton, 'but I get more money.'

Then they retreated to a special lunch prepared for them, where they knocked back around seventeen Martinis apiece. Elizabeth Taylor, who was there with Burton (but not for much longer), wanted to renew her acquaintance with Marvin with whom she'd worked in *Raintree County*. She came over to him, by which time he was in too much of a haze even to recognize her. He told her, 'Why don't you just fuck off, sweetie.'

Burton rose in anger, but Liz Taylor simply smiled at Marvin and said, 'I see you haven't changed a bit, Lee,' and walked off.

Director Terence Young was delighted to find that the two actors seemed intent on working seriously – except for Marvin's first scene which followed a boozy lunch and featured an equally boozy Marvin. After that Marvin managed to avoid drinking until the evening. Burton also restricted his drinking to the evening. But both of them, when they did hit the liquor, hit it hard. Though not necessarily together; they were not drinking buddies.

Shortly after the film began, Liz Taylor decided enough was enough. This was her second-time marriage to Burton, and he had promised her he'd give up drinking, but he had failed to keep his word, so she left. He began drinking even more and was clearly very ill. He coughed badly, he trembled and his eyes were bloodshot.

When one day nobody could rouse him from his trailer, it was Lee Marvin who entered quietly and found a sombre, lonely, sad man. In his own inimitable way, Marvin soon had Burton laughing, telling stories and singing Welsh songs for the rest of the day.

Burton was physically falling apart, and finally a doctor was called for. He examined Burton and announced, 'This man is dying. He'll be dead in three weeks.'

His kidneys were diseased but cirrhosis of the liver had not yet set in. His only chance was to have a complete blood transfusion. But there was just one last scene for Burton to complete before he could be hospitalized: his death scene. Young looked at Burton on the set and said to the make-up man, 'You've done a great job.'

'I haven't done anything to him yet,' replied the make-up artist.

The scene completed, a car took Burton straight to the airport and he was flown to Los Angeles and admitted to hospital. He received blood transfusions and tests, and lay seriously ill for a week. They managed to save him, giving him ten more years of life until he died aged fifty-nine in 1984.

As for Lee Marvin, he eventually gave up the hard liquor. In 1976 in London while he was making *Shout at the Devil*, he told me, 'I've been burning myself out. I'm finished with the drink. The aggressive, hard-living son-of-a-bitch Lee Marvin is no more. It's been getting too frightening. Work is important to me. Just be on time, hit the lines and say the marks!'

In Lee Marvin's last years, work became less important to him. He could afford to take it easy and he picked and chose carefully whatever he wanted to do. I was involved in the development of the script for a project he was keen to do. But he wasn't in a hurry and put the property on the shelf for a while. Before the screenplay could be completed Lee died, in 1987, aged sixty-three, having spent his last years living peacefully in Arizona, far away from the madness of Hollywood.

One of the very first actors to be labelled a hellraiser was Peter Finch. The son of an Australian physicist, he was born in London but made his name initially in several Australian movies and came back to London in 1949 as a protégé of Laurence Olivier.

He always rejected the hellraiser label but he began living up to his image when, in 1953, he embarked on a drunken affair with Vivien Leigh while filming *Elephant Walk* in Ceylon. Paramount had originally sent Olivier the screenplay, offering him and his wife Vivien Leigh the leads. Olivier turned it down flat and tried to persuade Vivien to do likewise. It was at Olivier's suggestion that producer Irving Asher cast Peter Finch in the male lead, while Vivien Leigh decided to ignore her husband's advice and accepted Paramount's offer.

Leigh had made it clear to Olivier during this time of her mental illness that she no longer loved him, and Olivier was well aware that his wife wanted to be with Finchie. On location in Ceylon, Vivien and Peter Finch would go off at 2 o'clock in the morning to celebrate. Finch was totally infatuated with her and they both put away vast quantities of alcohol between them.

But it was quickly becoming clear to all working on the film that Vivien was unwell. Her behaviour was becoming erratic. As for Peter, his marriage to Tamara, a ballet dancer, was in trouble, and he moved in with Vivien who seemed intent on flaunting their affair, to the embarrassment of the producer.

When Vivien appeared on the set badly made-up, with her wig perched ridiculously high on her head and refusing to alter a single thing, Asher reluctantly called Olivier and told him of the problems. Olivier flew straight out while Asher discreetly told Finch that it would be a good idea if he moved out of Vivien's room. When Olivier arrived she seemed somehow rejuvenated and filming continued. But by the time they were back in Hollywood to do interiors at Paramount Studios, she deteriorated and had to be replaced by Elizabeth Taylor.

Finchie, meanwhile, was spending a good deal of his time at Oblatz, a bar-restaurant just across the street from the studio. Then his own wife and daughter joined him in Hollywood, and he began to settle down again. His affair with Vivien Leigh was over.

In 1955 Warner Bros cast Peter in an Errol Flynn swashbuckler, *Dark Avenger*. As a fellow Australian and all-round boozer, Flynn took a tremendous liking to Finch, and, not surprisingly, they spent a good deal of time drinking together. Finch conceded that they drank 'far too much', bringing filming to a halt. But it wasn't unprofessionalism that caused Finchie to behave so uncharacteristically. Finch disapproved of Flynn coming to work in such a state, but when drunken Flynn caused chaos on the set, Finch knew that the fading swashbuckler was incapable of filming for that day, so he would join Flynn for a drink and a sing-song.

If fact, if it hadn't been for Finch's increasing drinking problem, he himself would never have behaved on the set in anything other than a professional way. But by the time he came to make *Josephine and Men* shortly after his film with Flynn, director Roy Boulting saw how he was going downhill.

Arriving at the studio at eight o'clock one morning, Boulting saw Finch staggering about the set drunk. Finch was due to start shooting a romantic scene with Glynis Johns at nine, but he was incapable and his eyes were bloodshot. The cameraman advised Boulting to shoot around Finch until lunch time.

With his brother John, who was producing, Roy Boulting tore Finch off a strip for holding up filming. 'This morning will cost you £500 out of your salary,' said Boulting.

Finch looked at him, smiled and said, 'You are absolutely right. I was bloodly awful. A disgrace! Please forgive me.'

As a major star during the late thirties and early forties, Errol Flynn was handsome and athletic . . .

. . . but by the time he was married to his third wife, Patrice Wymore, drink and drugs had aged and bloated him.

Chaplin was thirty-five when he married sixteen-year-old Lita Grey. His passion for young girls got him into trouble throughout much of his life.

John Gilbert's marriage to his fourth and final wife, Virginia Bruce, ended in 1934, two years before he drank himself to death.

The horrendously marked face of W C Fields reveals the ravages of years of drink.

John Barrymore was the silent screen's *Beloved Rogue* in 1927, but died a hopeless drunk.

Bobby Driscoll was Walt Disney's nine-year-old star of *Song of the South*, but spent some of his later years behind bars for drug offences.

The Mexican half of Anthony Quinn (seen here in *Guns for San Sebastian*) often resulted in brawls, including one with the US Marines. (*MGM*)

Yul Brynner dressed in black – his favourite colour – for *The Bounty Hunters* had an egotistical streak that upset some of his co-stars. (*United Artists*)

Two legendary hellraisers, Richard Burton and Peter O'Toole, appeared together in *Becket*. (*Paramount Pictures*)

Dennis Hopper (left), seen here with Nicholas Ray, became a drug culture star in the late sixties.

Peter Finch, seen here with Kim Novak in *The Legend of Lylah Clare*, loved wine and women. (*MGM*)

Director Roman Polanski and his tragic wife Sharon Tate, who was murdered in 1969. Several years later Polanski was charged with drugging and raping a thirteen-year-old girl, and consequently fled America to escape imprisonment.

The Boultings couldn't help but forgive him. As Roy said, 'How can you feel anything but deep affection for a man who has the humility and sincerity not to try and bluff it out?'

After his divorce from Tamara, he married Yolande Turnball on 4 July 1959. He had married her against all his friends' advice. He was infatuated with her. Now began a new phase of his life in which he tried to live a grand, filmstar-type life in a huge house on three acres of land. He hated it. He preferred Chelsea and being with his friends. His drinking increased.

He became so bored by family life (Tamara had given him a daughter and Yolande a son and a daughter) that he lost interest in his children. He was also bored with Yolande and started bringing home girls, suggesting to Yolande that they try a threesome. He was having a 'surfeit of sex and grog because I had temporarily lost the power to *feel*'.

In 1962, while he was filming *In the Cool of the Day* at MGM's Elstree Studios, the hired chauffeur often found himself having to drive Finchie home dead drunk from a night of wild passion. Sometimes Finch would leave Yolande in the morning for the studio and not return for several days.

Yolande divorced Peter in 1965 for adultery – the other party was named as Shirley Bassey.

He began seeing a Hollywood writer, Florrie Christmas, whom he took to Jamaica, where he drank himself into a stupor daily. Friends feared that he was killing himself.

Indeed, in 1973 he told Bertie Whiting, a close friend and best man at his wedding to his third and last wife Eletha, 'I'm not going to live long.' His heart was playing up, beating irregularly. His doctor told him he had to give up cigarettes and alcohol. Of course, he defied doctor's orders, and in 1977 he died of a massive heart attack, aged sixty.

Finch always maintained that he was never a hellraiser and that his image was wishful publicity by the press. Certainly, in comparison to Errol Flynn's, Finch's antics were mild. He didn't get into fights and he didn't try taking a bite at every sexual activity. But womanizing and drinking to the extent he did was not the behaviour of a mild-mannered man.

Trevor Howard too spurned his image of hellraiser. 'I never raised hell, amigo,' he once told me. 'I just like to enjoy myself, that's all.'

And enjoy himself he did. Usually with a drink or several and the company of good friends. Acting, he told me, was 'a wonderful job that gives me the opportunity to drink with some really good friends in exotic places around the world'. His friend Patrick Newell told me rather more about his drinking exploits.

> He did go out a lot. But he went out for three days, never for an hour and a quarter. Some years ago I said to him, 'I live on Mikonos now.'
>
> He said, 'I've been there. I went to Fulham Road years ago with a friend of mine and we ended up on Mikonos for ten days.'
>
> Bernard Lee [who played M in the Bond films] was a good friend of Trevor's. They used to do some outrageous things together when they'd had a couple of beers. Like they'd crawl across the floor in restaurants pretending to be a couple of dogs. Bernie would go 'Woof! Woof!' and Trevor would bark back, 'Get off, amigo!' But I never heard Trevor embarrass anyone, even if he'd had one or two.
>
> He used to say he could drink quite a bit because he had very low blood pressure. That was his excuse. I never bothered to look it up or ask anybody if that was true, but he'd say, 'I've got very low blood pressure so it doesn't matter how much I drink.'
>
> He could drink for twenty-four hours without stopping, but it was not done in a hurry. I remember one day we were at the studio doing *The Long Duel* and we obviously weren't going to work. We'd been in make-up and when we weren't called he said, 'Right, Dennis, open the bar.'

We sat there and had two or three or four and it got to 11 o'clock and we had a few sandwiches and things like that, and we just sat there talking. Then he said, 'Well, we're not going to work today, amigo. I think it's time we had a drink. I'll have a large whisky.'

And we sat there and talked until 12 o'clock at night, and his driver was asleep on the sofa in the hall outside. But Trevor always arrived in the morning as if he'd not had a drink.

I sat one night at Pinewood Studios with him right until make-up call the next day while he spoke about Errol Flynn the entire time. He absolutely worshipped Errol Flynn. I don't think many people ever realized that his biggest hero of all time was Flynn [with whom Howard worked in *The Roots of Heaven* in 1958].

They became great friends and when they did that film in Africa they had a 15-hundredweight truck behind them absolutely full of whisky that followed them everywhere they went.

Trevor was not the sort of fellow who said, 'For art's sake have I broken up the bar.' Not that sort of man at all. Oh, he slipped off the old bar stool occasionally and when going home tripped over the odd stone that he was sure wasn't there when he went out. But he wasn't like some I could mention – never that sort of noisy, knocking-it-down guy.

Actually, Trevor could get more than a little noisy. 'He was famous for his *roar*,' said Newell. 'The Trevor Howard Roar. He used to come through the doors of a restaurant with a loud "Whoooaaa!" Mainly in small Greek restaurants in the Fulham Road.'

Harry Andrews, who knew him for years, said, 'When he'd had a few drinks he could be noisy. If he was really pissed he was a roarer!'

Although never a trouble-maker, Trevor's drinking did get him into strife – and jail – on occasions. While making *Mutiny on the Bounty* in Tahiti, the megrims of working with Marlon Brando drove him to drink more than usual. Along with the rest of the British actors he drowned his sorrows each evening at the island's taverns. One late night they all returned to their homes but Trevor was missing. No one knew where he was.

The next morning at 7.30 the cast and crew were called to board the *Bounty* for filming at sea. Trevor was nowhere in sight. An hour and a half later a police wagon pulled up at the dock, and out from the back climbed a bleary-eyed Howard escorted by two gendarmes. He staggered up the gang-plank, waving goodbye to the policemen, and by the time the cameras were due to roll, he was in make-up and wardrobe ready for his first scene.

'Had a driving offence or two,' he once told me, 'but I never broke the law by smashing up pubs and restaurants. But I did get arrested while making *The Third Man* in Vienna.'

He went on to explain.

One evening I discovered a place which had a band, and I heard music coming from it and just couldn't resist it. Problem was I was playing a British Military Police Chief, and I still had my uniform on when I turned up at this place. In no time at all I was conducting the band, having a few drinks and thoroughly enjoying myself.

Some soldier saw me, realized I wasn't a real major and I suppose he thought I was impersonating an officer or whatever. Anyway, the silly bugger called the police and I was arrested.

The next morning someone from the production office turned up and said, 'Please can we have our actor back,' and they let me go.

The 'driving offence or two' Trevor referred to was more serious. In 1962 he was driving home following a drinking session to ease the tensions of recording a TV play, *Hedda Gabler*, when he crashed into some roadworks.

The police were quickly on the scene and had Trevor

walking up and down a straight line. He complained that they should be looking after him instead of making him do all 'this nonsense'. He appeared in court to answer a charge of drink-driving – not, it transpired, for the first time. He faced a prison sentence, and in his eagerness to keep his client out of prison, defending QC Mr Christmas Humphreys claimed that Trevor had been overworking and was drinking 'to give him the energy to carry on a task that was almost more than he could bear'. He assured the court that Howard was going to take a well-needed holiday as soon as he could.

The judge took a dim view of all this and told Howard, 'You are a man who drinks vast quantities every night. You have so little care for your fellow citizens that you are willing to drive.'

Nevertheless, the court decided that imprisonment would be in neither Howard's nor the public's interests, so he was fined £50, ordered to pay £30 costs and disqualified from driving for eight years. Consequently, for almost a decade after that, Trevor was never actually seen driving a car in any film.

But he didn't stop drinking on or off the set.

He never had much regard for the damage drinking could cause him, yet oddly enough he did about others. 'Once I met him in the local pub,' Patrick Newell recalled. 'The chap who ran it was ill upstairs with "publican's disease". Trevor said, "I'm just going upstairs to see him. He's in bed. He drinks too much, damn fool that he is."

'He went upstairs and gave the landlord a terrible reading about drinking. "You shouldn't do that. It's very bad for you. You'll kill youself if you go on drinking like that."

'But he never stopped to think about how much he drank.'

In his own defence, Trevor said, 'I know I drink too much but that helps me to give the kind of performance I think the public wants.' And he managed to live until he was seventy-one, much longer than the expectancy of any hellraiser, although in the end it was the drinking that took him in 1988.

He had his beloved wife Helen by his side in the last days

and hours of his life. Howard's friend and drinking buddy, William Holden, was less fortunate in his final moments. He died drunk and alone in 1983, a victim of his own temperament and the trappings of being a Hollywood star. Not that Holden was disliked. Far from it. But he drank alone and often.

A tense, private man, he rarely gave interviews. When *Photoplay*'s editor Ken Ferguson went down to the set of *The Devil's Brigade*, a World War Two adventure filmed in England in 1968, he and the other reporters were warned not to try and interview the star. Ferguson recollected what happened.

Holden seemed particularly nervous, repeating his lines over and over to himself like a raw newcomer terribly afraid he might forget how to deliver when the time came. The invited press corps kept its distance from Holden, leaving him in peace to concentrate on his performance. But later in the day, after most of the press had gone, he actually came over to speak to me.

Quietly spoken, and with the tensions of his acting day behind him, Holden now seemed more relaxed and chatty. He didn't ask me who I was. I didn't tell him. If I had our impromptu interview would have been quickly and suddenly over.

Hollywood's Golden Boy was by 1968 an alcoholic who, like many another hellraiser, was sacrificing professionalism for booze. He was knocking back a bottle of vodka each morning while he was making *The Devil's Brigade*.

One day he went missing, and the producer went in search of him, eventually catching sight of his Rolls-Royce parked outside a bar. Inside was Holden, smashed.

The Holden temperament was let loose on location in Italy when locals came to watch the filming, sitting on a bridge while Holden and other members of the cast waded through fast-flowing, freezing cold water. Suddenly Holden turned his machine-gun on the onlookers and fired, scattering them in all directions and scaring them to death even though he was only firing blanks.

These days it's becoming quite fashionable for hellraisers to reform. When I first met John Hurt in 1977, when he was in Devon filming *The Shout*, I saw at first hand how much he drank. During a lunch break I sat with him in a village pub where he put away a few pints. Then in the evening he sat in the ballroom of the hotel where the cast where staying, getting pissed on shorts. The producer's girlfriend kept getting John on to the dance floor, and the more John drank, the more intolerant he became of her. When she passed him the number of her room (thinking no one else knew she had) and left to await him, he remained in the ballroom drinking, and when I left at midnight he was still there looking bored and lonely, missing his live-in girlfriend Marie Lisa Volpelierre (who not long after died so tragically in a riding accident).

'I find life so boring if I cannot enjoy a drink,' he said. (It wasn't unknown for Hurt to go on four-day benders.) 'I notice details about what's going on around me,' he said in defence of his drinking. 'I am much more aware.'

He was also aware of the dangers. 'People who drink heavily are probably knocking twenty years off their lives.'

He claimed that drinking enhanced some of his performances. 'When I made *Midnight Express* I had to play a man who was in a permanent messed-up state. I was drinking seven [*seven?*] bottles of wine a day. When I portrayed Quentin Crisp in *The Naked Civil Servant* I was just evenly pissed throughout.

'*The Elephant Man* was a different approach entirely. I didn't touch a drop.'

When he appeared in the play *The Hunting of the Snark* at the Royal Albert Hall before the Duchess of York in 1987, he remained sober. He could go without when he wanted. Over the years he made numerous attempts to give up drinking altogether. 'I can give it up,' he said in 1987, 'but when I wake up in the morning, I actually think about drink. It's very difficult for Donna, my wife.'

By the time he had divorced Donna and married his third wife, Jo Dalton, in January 1990 (his first marriage to Annette Robertson ended in 1964), the fifty-year-old star had stopped drinking.

Peter O'Toole is another reformed character. Like *Lawrence of Arabia* going up and down the majestic sand dunes, he has over the years risen to great heights, and plummeted to great depths. 'You have to have the lows, the valleys,' he has said. 'The trudge is also an important part of life. The trouble with everyone these days is that they want constant sensation, to live on the peaks of existence.'

When he went from RADA to the Bristol Old Vic he was soon in trouble for drinking too much. Together, he and his long-time friend from their days at RADA, Richard Harris, seemed determined to out-drink each other. Now they are both firmly on the wagon.

'I can't remember what it's like to be drunk,' said O'Toole some years after taking the pledge, 'it's so long since a drink passed my lips. But I can remember when Richard Harris and me were skint students. We threw parties while travelling on the tube on the good old Central Line. Great days.'

Peter Finch was another of O'Toole's close friends with whom he liked to pull a cork. In 1964, while Finch was filming *Girl With Green Eyes* in Dublin, the two Peters found themselves being refused drinks in a pub at Bray because it was after hours. They decided therefore that the only way to get another drink was to buy the pub. They wrote out a cheque for the place there and then and became the owners of their own pub.

The next morning, realizing and regretting what they'd done, they went back to the pub and were relieved to discover that the publican hadn't cashed their cheque. He tore it up, and they all remained good friends until the day the publican died. O'Toole and Finch even attended his funeral but –

probably having drunk a little more than they'd meant to, to ease their grief – they found themselves at the wrong funeral and mourning over the wrong body being buried.

Harris, even after reforming, remained nostalgic about the good old days of drinking, much of it with his soul-mate from RADA, O'Toole, who was also his countryman (both were born in 1932 in Eire – O'Toole in Kerry and Harris in Limerick). 'The pure and simple fact', said Harris, 'is that I loved it.'

There was no other reason whatsoever. I adored getting drunk and I adored reading in the papers what I had done the night before.

When I was younger I had a sort of affinity with Peter O'Toole, but I didn't mix with actors much. Most of the guys I hung around with had nothing to do with the business. There was my brother Dermot who died in 1986. That was a big shock to me. He was my best pal and he died aged forty-six.

It was anybody I could pick on – anybody who could last the course. That was the great virtue of boozing, to go into a pub by yourself and end up with fifteen mates just for the night. Men. Not women. Boozing is a man's world. You can't have women there. You have too many obligations.

Richard Harris, who has also had the highs and lows in plenty, gave up drinking at exactly 11.20 pm on 11 August 1981 at the Jockey Club. He had been told by the doctors that he would be dead within a year if he didn't stop drinking. So Harris decided to go out in style.

He ordered two bottles of Château Margaux 1957, at $300 a bottle. He drank every last drop and then announced, 'I have finished my last glass.' He hasn't touched a drop since.

O'Toole always refused to say why and when he stopped drinking, but denied that it was because of a stomach operation he underwent.

With the sobering-up of these two legendary hellraisers came something like the end of an era. But one wild man of the movies refused to join the teetotal club, and continued flying the well-oiled flag – Oliver Reed.

By the time he reached his fifties, Ollie Reed had slowed down somewhat. Gone were the days when he smashed up hotels and pubs, dropped his trousers on an aeroplane and climbed up a pub chimney while the fire was still alight. But when he finishes a movie he is still apt to 'break out and go a bit mad. But that is in my own time and what I do in my own time is up to me.'

I've met Ollie Reed on two different film sets – *The Big Sleep* and *The Class of Miss MacMichael* – and it has to be said that he certainly appeared totally sober. However, during a break in filming *The Big Sleep* I did join him and Robert Mitchum for a drink at a nearby pub. Mitchum, of course, is another of the great boozers. Some might even call him a hellraiser. But Mitchum has rarely raised any kind of hell. He's a very quiet, private person, and on this day he and Ollie Reed were more concerned in refusing to answer any of my questions. They weren't so much being difficult as simply teasing, and it made for a very amusing if unproductive hour.

Both Mitchum and Reed refrain from getting drunk on film sets. 'You can't do half a dozen pages of dialogue if you're pissed,' said Reed. But he continues to drink away in his own private time and has no intention of following in the dry footsteps of O'Toole and Harris.

'I don't have a drink problem. But if that was the case and doctors told me I would have to stop drinking, I'd like to think I'd be brave enough to drink myself into the grave.

'Now that Richard Harris and Peter O'Toole have stopped drinking, they don't look nearly as robust as they used to. I certainly preferred them in their stamping days.'

There doesn't seem to be any great love lost between Reed and Harris, and even now Harris says, 'Oliver and I have never met but I'm a great admirer of his. I think he is a real talent gone to waste.

'I'll bet he couldn't have survived with the rest of us. I don't care how much he drank. He drinks beer, doesn't he? That's a poof drink. Mine was vodka. Two bottles a day. That would take me up to seven in the evening, then I'd break open a bottle of brandy and a bottle of port and mix them.'

Apart from Ollie Reed (and even he's slowing up) the hellraiser is dead. But there is another breed of contemporary hard-living actors and even they are having to rethink their lifestyle – the acid-dropping, cocaine-sniffing bums of Beverly Hills.

5

Reefer Rogues

On 31 August 1948 it seemed certain that another glorious Hollywood career was about to be poured down the drain when Robert Mitchum was arrested for smoking marijuana. Handcuffed and hauled off to the Los Angeles County jail, he was mug-photoed, fingerprinted and seemingly washed up. Nobody had ever survived a drugs bust in Hollywood. There was nothing to suggest Mitchum would be the exception to the rule.

His background hardly prepared him for a life of elegant luxury as a film star or obedience to the star system. He had had an unhappy home life as a child and his youth was marked by a certain amount of delinquency. His jobs included digging ditches, coal-mining and factory work. He also frisked drunks and got himself arrested on a vagrancy charge. He did a stint on a chain gang, and he became a professional boxer for a while.

Encouraged by his sister Julie, a night-club singer, he became an extra in films and graduated his way through a long succession of walk-ons to become a featured player in B-pictures. Then, while under contract to both RKO and David O Selznick, he was cast by director William Wellman as a tough army captain in *The Story of GI Joe* (1945), for which he was nominated for a Best Supporting Actor Oscar.

Dorothy Mitchum, his wife since 1940, tried to get him to move away from the West Coast after eight years of marriage, but he didn't want to leave so she and the children left him to go and live in New York. He hoped to entice her back by selling their old property and buying a new home. To help him find a buyer, he enlisted the help of one Robin 'Danny' Ford, a bartender with a side-line in insurance and real estate.

Friends had warned Mitchum to steer clear of this hustler, but they became close friends. One day at the beach, they encountered a beautiful blonde starlet called Lila Leeds, something of a Lana Turner lookalike. They gave her dinner and Mitchum took a fancy to her, suddenly forgetting all about his wife back East. He invited Lila for a night out on the town.

On 31 August Mitchum and Ford, after spending the day looking for property to buy, knocked back a number of whiskys between them. They were just getting into their stride when they received an invitation from Lila to come to her place. They arrived shortly after midnight, unaware that Lila's bungalow was being watched by two narcotics officers as part of an eight-month-old campaign engineered by Harry J Anslinger, Commissioner of the United States Treasury Bureau of Narcotics. The officers had been tipped off that a film idol was going to be a guest of Lila Leeds.

Mitchum and Ford were greeted by Lila who was wearing white shorts and a bathrobe. She introduced them to her room-mate Vicki Evans. Mitchum, wearing dark glasses, insisted the lights be dimmed, and then threw a packet of cigarettes on to the coffee table. Lila picked them up and examined the contents.

'Oh, you've got brown ones and white ones too,' she exclaimed, recognizing the brown ones as joints of marijuana. She took a joint from the pack, lit up and offered one to Mitchum who accepted. Just a little later Mitchum caught sight of two faces peering through the window. He leapt up and ran to the window, telling his friends what he'd seen. They advised him to stop mixing alcohol and dope.

The two officers outside, having spent a great deal of time and effort befriending the young boxer dogs Lila kept to ward off unwanted guests, scratched at the kitchen door in imitation of the dogs. Vicki opened the door, expecting to be bounded at by boisterous dogs. To her horror she came face to face with the two officers standing there with guns drawn. She was the only one who had not lit up. The other three were caught with the joints in their hands. One of the officers picked up the packet from the coffee table and counted fifteen more joints. Then he picked up the phone and called for additional officers.

At the county jail Mitchum and his friends were booked. Asked if he had any identifying marks he pulled up his sleeve and pointed to a tiny tattoo of an obscene word.

Asked if he'd ever been arrested before, Mitchum replied, 'Only for speeding, drunkenness and disorderly conduct.'

He was stripped naked, shackled and questioned by a psychiatrist. The shrink asked Mitchum what he liked doing at parties.

'I get drunk, follow the pretty broads, make a fool of myself and stagger home,' said Mitchum.

Did he ever go out with pretty girls? He replied, 'No.'

'Why not?' asked the psychiatrist.

'Because,' said Mitchum, 'my wife won't let me.'

Sergeant Barr of the Los Angeles police announced to the gathered reporters: 'We're going to clean the dope and the narcotics users out of Hollywood. And we don't care who we're going to have to arrest. This is only the beginning of a Hollywood clean-up.'

When the press were allowed to interview the star-spangled jailbird, Mitchum said, 'Yes, boys, I was smoking a marijuana cigarette when they came in.' Concerning his prison clothes, he said, 'Sorry my new outfit doesn't appeal to you, fellows. It doesn't appeal to me either.' Joking aside, he was depressed at his prospects and said, 'Well, this is the bitter end of everything – my career, my home, my marriage.'

A few hours later famed attorney to the stars Jerry Geisler was called in to defend Mitchum and warned him to say nothing more.

Meanwhile David O Selznick made a public plea for people not to judge Mitchum until the courts had done so. He was, said Selznick, 'a very sick man in need of medical treatment instead of a lawbreaker'. Mitchum was furious when he heard that.

Mitchum, Ford and Lila were given bail at a thousand dollars each and a hearing was scheduled for the following week. Mitchum sought seclusion in his mother's home.

Not surprisingly, the press turned the case into a trial-by-newspaper. The *St Louis Globe-Democrat* wrote, 'Now we have a young swoon actor, the idol of teenagers, caught in a marijuana party – a reefer smoking fest known to the trade as "kicking the gong around".'

The hideous Hollywood hack Hedda Hopper was uncharacteristically liberal in her views. 'If it is proved before a jury of his peers that Robert Mitchum violated the law, he must be made to pay the penalty just like any other citizen, rich or poor, famous or a nobody. That is the American way.

'However – and it is a BUT in capital letters – it's as deplorable as it's inevitable that because he happens to be a movie star his actions have drawn a torrent of destructive attention upon the entire industry with a free-for-all splurge in 57 varieties of scandal, malicious tongue-wagging and dirt.'

There were calls for Mitchum's movies to be banned. He had a new film ready for release, *Rachel and the Stranger*. RKO decided to chance its release. To their immense relief and great pleasure it played to capacity audiences. The fans still loved their idol, and Mitchum could now afford to relax and believe that his studio would not find itself forced to invoke the 'morals clause' and thus cancel his contract.

The District Attorney decided to call for a grand jury inquiry and invited Mitchum and the other defendants to attend. Geisler advised Mitchum against accepting the invitation, as did the other defendants' lawyers.

The DA had the only two witnesses available – the two narcotics officers who made the bust. Their testimony was purely to establish that the substance they had seized was marijuana. After two hours, Mitchum, Ford, Leeds and Vicki Evans were indicted on two counts: possession of marijuana and conspiracy to violate the State Narcotics Act.

The defendants, with the exception of Vicki Evans, who jumped bail and fled to New York, appeared in court on 29 September to enter their pleas. Geisler attempted to bring about a delay in the proceedings on a technicality: the term *Cannabis sativa* used in the indictments is Latin, and the law required that all indictments should be couched in English. Judge Ambrose overruled.

When asked how he pleaded, Mitchum replied, 'Not guilty.' The other two defendants pleaded likewise. Their trial was slated for 23 November but it was postponed until 10 January 1949 because Geisler broke three ribs in a car crash and was unfit to appear.

Howard Hughes and his RKO production team decided to rush Mitchum into a star vehicle. As well as cashing in on the publicity, Hughes hoped the judge might be persuaded to grant Mitchum parole or postpone his jail term – if it came to that – until he had finished the film. *The Big Steal* was a shelved George Raft vehicle. Now it was a Robert Mitchum quickie. It went before the cameras on 4 January 1949. Everyone knew it was a piece of junk, made for the sole purpose of making a quick buck and maybe keeping Mitchum out of jail. The cast and crew were prepared to plant their tongues in their cheeks and work hard.

Mitchum and Geisler arrived for the trial, surrounded by frenzied fans. Mitchum-mania was at its zenith. Geisler and the other two defending lawyers proposed that the two counts be severed and that the people's case consist of a reading of the 32-page grand jury transcript. The motion was granted and the trial began.

The three defendants were found guilty of conspiracy to possess drugs. 9 February was set for sentencing. Geisler applied for probation for Mitchum and a further hearing was set for February. As they left the courtroom Ford tried to speak to Mitchum, but Geisler barred his way. In answer to the reporters' questions as to why he hadn't put up a defence for Mitchum, Geisler said, 'The evidence was in the transcript. And Mr Mitchum wouldn't perjure himself. He would have to tell the truth.'

Mitchum was sentenced to a year in the county jail. Then the judge suspended the sentence, placing him on probation for two years but with the first sixty days to be spent in Los Angeles County Jail. He became prisoner number 91234. His cell contained a steel bunk with a thin mattress, a wash basin and a toilet. 'I've slept in worse,' he said. There were no special privileges for the Hollywood star. He joined every other prisoner in the mess hall for breakfast each morning at six-thirty. Then he returned to his cell to sweep and mop it. He bore it all with bright spirits and was never anything less than an exemplary prisoner.

He even posed for the newspaper photographers, insisting only that they refrain from taking behind-the-bars type pictures. 'I want everything as upbeat as possible for the kids' sake,' he said. He even later posed with the warden.

Life in the slammer wasn't too bad for Bob Mitchum. His prediction that his marriage was over didn't come to pass. Dorothy stood by him and came to visit him every day. He was made a trusty and the other prisoners got on well with him. So when he s told he was going to be transferred to the Sheriff's Wayside Honor Farm at Castaic, he told reporters, 'I've been pretty happy in the tank here. And I'm really proud that the men in the tank recommended me to the jailers to be the trusty. That's considered quite an honour. No, I'm not happy about leaving.'

In his new jail, Mitchum was put to work in the cement plant. The heavy labour not only fought the flab around his waist but cured him of the insomnia he had suffered from for so many years. Then the officials decided to transfer him back to the Los Angeles County Jail. When asked how he had enjoyed his stay at Castaic, he said, 'It was a relief to get away for a while. It's the first vacation I've had in seven years. I worked hard, slept well, and believe it or not, batted eight hundred on The Rancho softball team. We won the last eight games. That farm's just like a weekend in Palm Springs – a great place to get in shape. Only you meet a better class of people.'

A week later, on 30 March, Mitchum and Lila Leeds were released on probation. They never met again, for under the probationary terms they were forbidden to associate with each other.

Mitchum emerged with his popularity intact and as RKO's biggest star. David O Selznick no longer owned a part of him. Howard Hughes had bought Selznick's half of Mitchum's contract.

He was the first star to weather the storm of a dope scandal, emerging unscathed and proving the *Indianapolis Star* wrong when it prophesied that 'The public never did – never will – laugh off a dope scandal involving a screen favourite performer. It was a resounding narcotics sensation that first threatened the film industry with obliteration back in 1920 when the handsome Wallace Reid, a public idol created by *The Birth of a Nation*, ran afoul of federal authorities.'

But times, morals and attitudes had changed radically since 1922 (the *Indianapolis Star* also got the year wrong) when Wally Reid, the 'King of Parmount', was placed in a sanatorium to be treated for drug abuse.

Wallace Reid was a victim of fame, the star system, a drugs dealer and of Will H Hays, the first movie censor. In his quest for a good time, Reid partied and drank his way through his considerable salary. But his introduction to drugs came from the Paramount doctor who, under orders from studio boss Adolph Zukor, started pumping morphine into Reid to keep him working after he had suffered head injuries in a train crash in 1919. The frequent doses led to his addiction. A bit-part actor from the Sennett lot made extra money by servicing movie stars with drugs, and he gave Reid his first fix for free.

Hays had been called in to clean up Hollywood following the wave of scandals which began when Roscoe 'Fatty' Arbuckle was tried for rape and manslaughter, and continued with the murder of William Desmond Taylor. Taylor was one of the men who was supposed to be responsible for cleaning up Hollywood, but as the sordid details of his life came to light during the murder investigation, Will Hays, knowing he could trust no one in the movie business, placed spies everywhere. No film star, director, or anyone connected with the business, knew for sure who was hiding where and checking on their lives and loves. Until, that was, Hays had his Doom Book compiled, featuring 117 'unsafe' names. Among them was Wallace Reid because of his drug addiction.

This was a further blow for Adolph Zukor; both Arbuckle and Taylor had been under contract to him. Zukor had risked a great deal in his cover-up of evidence in the Taylor scandal, and he was not going to go through another nightmare, so he decided to have Reid put away. He persuaded Reid's wife, actress Dorothy Davenport, to sign Wally's commitment papers which put him into a private sanatorium. Paramount publicly claimed Reid was suffering from 'overwork' and needed to recover. Mrs Wallace Reid, however, told the press the truth – that her husband was having treatment for morphine addiction.

America was shocked. There was an outcry against Hollywood, the very thing Hays and Zukor had tried to avoid. Hays attempted to calm things down, stating that 'the unfortunate Mr Reid should be dealt with as a diseased person – not be censured or shunned'.

Wally Reid was actually keen to kick the habit. But instead of allowing himself to be weaned off the drug, he went 'cold turkey'. It affected his mind, or so it was said; he became paranoid and was obsessed with the thought that he had been used as a scapegoat. This bout of 'insanity' led to his being placed in a padded cell. He remained there until he died on 18 January 1923, aged thirty.

A vengeful Mrs Wallace Reid turned over to police all the

names of those she believed had been responsible for Wally's debauched lifestyle. These men referred to themselves as the 'Hollywood Hellraisers'. Reid's widow called them 'Bohemians'.

'Gradually he got to drinking with his Bohemian friends,' she said, 'and soon this wasn't a home. It was a roadhouse. Wally's friends would come in here by the scores, at any odd hour of the day or night. They came, they stayed, they drank. It was one wild party after another, each one worse than the last. Nobody could do anything with Wally. And then morphine.'

She added, 'Wally was cured, but terribly debilitated physically. Only a return to the drug under control could have saved him. He refused.'

With Will Hay's backing, she starred in a film that exposed drug trafficking, *Human Wreckage*. It didn't deter many of Hollywood's young stars in those days of silent movies from using drugs. Barbara La Marr, Alma Rubens and Juanita Hansen were just some of the stars whose drug addiction ended either their lives or their careers, whichever came first.

For Walt Disney's child-star Bobby Driscoll from *Song of the South*, there was to be no long-term future. In 1946, Bobby Driscoll, then only nine years old, listened to the remarkable stories of Br'er Rabbit as told by Uncle Remus in that enchanting Disney film. He was also Jim Hawkins in Disney's *Treasure Island* in 1950, and he supplied the animated Peter Pan with a voice.

Unlike Peter Pan, Bobby was in too much of a hurry to grow up. He was just seventeen when he began experimenting with drugs, shooting heroin into his arm. Two years later he was married, and not long after he and a friend were busted in his home for possession of narcotics. He avoided jail but found that the studios were avoiding him, though he did managed to land a leading role in a B-picture, *The Party Crashers* in 1958. It was his last picture.

Shortly after, he was arrested for possession of heroin. The police found needle marks up his arm. In 1960 he was in trouble with the law again when a crowd of youths began taunting him as he washed a friend's car. He pulled out a gun and, according to his testimony, one of the youths 'bumped into the gun'.

From 1961 there was a succession of arrests: for breaking into an animal clinic, for forging a stolen cheque, and on several drugs busts. In court he said, 'I had everything. I was earning more than $50,000 a year, working steadily with good parts. Then I started putting all my spare time in my arm ... Now no one will hire me because of my arrests.'

He was sentenced to six months at the Narcotics Rehabilitation Center of the Chino State Penitentiary. 'I'm looking forward to the coming months at Chino,' he said. In prison he didn't have to worry about where his next meal was coming from.

In 1965, unable to get any work in Hollywood, he moved to New York and drifted around the Lower East Side, cadging money to buy drugs.

In October 1969 Driscoll's mother called the Disney Studios. Bobby's father was dying and she couldn't trace their son. The FBI had failed to find him. She was desperate for their help. Disney hired a Los Angeles law agency to seek Driscoll out.

Flashback to 30 March 1968: two kids playing in a deserted tenement block discover a corpse. The body carries no identification. A post mortem reveals methedrine in the bloodstream. The body is fingerprinted and buried in a pauper's grave on Hart Island.

In the search for Bobby Driscoll the law agency began having his fingerprints matched with every deceased 'John Doe'. Two weeks after Driscoll's father died, Bobby's fingerprints were finally matched with the body found by the two kids.

In 1972 *Song of the South* was reissued. His mother told the press, 'He was such a fine boy. Please tell people that no woman ever had a finer, more generous son. Drugs changed him. He didn't bathe, his teeth got loose. He had an extremely high IQ, but the narcotics affected his brain.'

Most stars managed to hide their addiction from the public eye. Errol Flynn's drug abuse was only revealed after his death. The same was true of Monroe. In more recent times drugs have been used more frequently and not just by the stars. Dope and cocaine have become accessible to the grips, the gaffers and the best boys.

During the sixties and seventies there were a good many 'hip' stars smoking dope and dropping acid, emulating their counterparts in rock music. During the eighties, and now during the nineties, more and more stars, directors and behind-the-scenes boys, have turned to using cocaine, Angel Dust and other substances that are stronger, harder and more dangerous than marijuana.

Dennis Hopper's life reflects Hollywood's drug problem over the past three decades. As a nineteen-year-old raw would-be rebel in 1954, he made his movie début opposite James Dean in *Rebel Without a Cause*. Hopper and Dean had much in common. Both grew up in the lonely forties, and both were nonconformists. They were joined, to a lesser extent, by Nick Adams, later to star in TV's *The Rebel*. He idolized James Dean, and also worked with him in *Rebel Without a Cause*.

These rebels felt they had a cause. As Dennis Hopper said, 'When I first arrived in Hollywood in 1954, Sunset Strip was all black ties and Rolls-Royces. You couldn't go into a restaurant on The Strip if you didn't have a black tie. We thought that was ridiculous. We had our own ideals and we wanted room to stretch our talents.'

Dean was making it as a star before Hopper was. Even Nick Adams did well for himself – at first. After *Rebel Without a Cause* Hopper played supporting roles in several films including *Gunfight at the OK Corral* and *The Steel Jungle*, while Dean landed his third starring role in *Giant*. Hopper won a supporting role in that film too. But when Dean died before the film was completed, Hopper quit Hollywood in a fit of drunken depression and headed for New York and Lee Strasberg's Actors' Studio.

The sixties became the decade of Dennis Hopper, but only towards the end of it. The first years of that decade were spent largely making B-pictures and westerns. But in 1968 he somehow persuaded Columbia to let him direct *Easy Rider*. The film's free-spirited, dope-promoting, flower-powered, born-to-be-wild philosophy mirrored Hopper's own lifestyle. His first of three wives, Brooke Hayward, recently described his Oscar-nominated performance as a drug-dealing gangster in *Blue Velvet* as 'the way you would have seen Dennis behaving any number of nights in the sixties'.

It was in the year of *Easy Rider* that Nick Adams was found dead. He had looked all set to succeed James Dean with his hit TV series *The Rebel*. He won further prestige when he was nominated for an Oscar as Best Supporting Actor for *Twilight of the Gods* in 1963. But suddenly it all started to go wrong for him. The TV series was cancelled, and Adams found himself making ridiculous Japanese B-films like *Frankenstein Conquers the World* and awful Godzilla monster movies.

Either sick, or just drunk, he was prescribed paraldehyde, a drug used to treat alcoholics with the DTs. On 7 February 1968 he failed to meet a friend, who was worried enough to call at Adams's house on El Roble in Beverly Hills to find out what had happened to him. There he found Adams dead. Thomas Noguchi, Hollywood's most celebrated mortician, found the prescribed drug in the organs, 'mixed with sedatives and other drugs – enough to cause instant death'.

Having outlived Dean and Adams, Hopper indulged himself during the early seventies in autobiographical ego trips that nobody went to see like *The Last Movie* and *The American Dreamer*. The sixties were gone and Hopper was just a memory. In 1979 he appeared in Coppola's *Apocalypse Now*, but his career didn't really begin to pick up again until he checked into Cedar-Sinai Medical Center's drug abuse programme in 1984. Since then he has returned to the

Hollywood fold in a big way, starring in numerous films and directing *Colors*.

'I can't change my past,' he says, 'but I can have a damn good try at the future. I've found that my perception of acting and movie-making has changed drastically since I hung up my addiction, and I've finally realized what damage I was doing to my career. I finally realized that I've got to live with that. And what's more damaging is that everything I do now will always be compared to the past.'

Richard Dreyfuss once looked like an actor who could do no wrong. He appeared to have the Midas Touch. By the age of twenty-nine he had appeared in two of the most successful films of all time and had won an Oscar for *The Goodbye Girl*. He could have been forgiven for thinking that he was God's gift to acting. But nobody could overlook the fact that the box-office receipts for *Jaws* and *Close Encounters of the Third Kind* had little to do with any *actor's* presence. But Hollywood is fickle and the success of *Jaws* made Dreyfuss a huge star. 'After *Jaws* I could have pissed in a pot and they would have paid me something,' he says.

But because in Hollywood you're only as good as your last movie, things started to go sour for Dreyfuss after starring in *The Big Fix*, a big flop. Then came *The Competition*, from the set of which filtered reports of tantrums, culminating in Dreyfuss hating the finished film so much that he refused to promote it.

Whose Life Is It, Anyway? gave Dreyfuss his finest performance as a paraplegic fighting for the right to die. But audiences didn't care if the film died. Then he lost out to Roy Scheider for the lead in Bob Fosse's *All That Jazz*, and he turned down *Arthur* which remains Dudley Moore's most famous film.

Dreyfuss became increasingly self-destructive. In 1982, while under the influence of drugs and alcohol, he rolled his Mercedes in a 100 m.p.h. crash which he miraculously survived. He was arrested, charged with possession of cocaine and only just missed serving a jail sentence when the court ordered him to attend a drugs rehabilitation centre. The rehabilitated star is once again in his orbit, making movies virtually back to back instead of not making movies because he was *on* his back.

Television's 'Hammer' found himself in the slammer when he tried smuggling cocaine into Britain a few years back. Stacy Keach, a far more versatile actor than his many mundane films would have you believe, was busted at Heathrow Airport and served three months of a nine-month sentence at Reading Jail.

For him, doing time was in itself a rehabilitating experience. 'I didn't particularly enjoy being a guest of Her Majesty but the experience gave me the chance to get my priorities straight,' he said.

His priorities included divorcing his wife Jill Donahue and marrying twenty-nine-year-old Polish actress Malgosia Tomasi. He also quit cocaine, busying himself by working in the prison library. Apparently his fellow jailbirds were also a tonic. 'Sometimes I was in the depths of despair, but the other inmates helped to carry me through prison.'

Other Hollywood stars caught red-handed by Heathrow's ever-vigilant Customs and Excise men include Tony Curtis. The bust was an acute embarrassment to Curtis who, in 1970, was the anti-smoking lobby's most famous disciple. He had arrived in England with his wife Lesley to begin filming the TV series *The Persuaders* when customs discovered an ounce of cannabis resin hidden in his shaving kit.

He was taken straight to West Drayton police station and charged with possession of drugs. The next day he appeared at the Uxbridge Magistrates' Court where he admitted having the drug in his possession. His lawyer, Mr Geoffrey Leach, told the court, 'He does not smoke cannabis. A friend seeing him off from New York on Sunday gave him this to relieve the tension he might face here. He noticed the accused was looking strained and worried. He is staying here for at least a year to make a television series with Roger Moore.'

Whether this struck some kind of patriotic chord or there

were some powers at work behind the scenes, Curtis was merely fined £50.

He told the press, 'Everyone has been truly wonderful to me. I discharged my responsibility at the court, and that is that. Let the past be the past.'

Three major TV networks immediately cancelled his anti-smoking commercials.

Mr Leach had told the court that Curtis had been a staunch supporter of the anti-smoking campaign and that his father had died from lung cancer. What he didn't say was that during his father's last days in 1958 Tony gave him marijuana to ease the pain.

As Hollywood history has shown, Curtis recognized that he did have a drug problem when, in 1984, he admitted himself into the Betty Ford Alcoholic and Drugs Treatment Center for treatment for his drug abuse and alcoholism.

Anthony Perkins, too, fell foul of the law in Great Britain. Nobody would have known that he was planning to puff on home-grown cannabis in Wales if it hadn't been for the ironic coincidence that another Mr Perkins had mistakenly opened a package addressed to the actor.

Anthony Perkins, the star of *Psycho*, had grown his own cannabis back home in Los Angeles and had thought to avoid being busted by customs by posting it to the hotel in Wales where he was due to stay in June 1989. But in a severe case of mistiming, or just underestimating the efficiency of the postal service, the package arrived five days before he did.

Opened by another Mr Perkins who was staying at the same hotel, the package was passed to police who were ready and waiting for the actor when he arrived at the hotel in Cardiff. He was fined £200 by Cardiff magistrates for smuggling in 1.32 grammes of cannabis. The court heard how he intended to use the drug to help him relax while filming for HTV in South Wales. The cannabis was worth only £4.50 and would have made no more than six cigarettes. 'He uses cannabis very infrequently and always discreetly,' said his solicitor.

But this wasn't the first time Perkins had been charged with drug possession in Britain. Five years earlier he had been fined £100 by magistrates at Uxbridge for trying to smuggle cannabis and LSD through customs at Heathrow Airport.

For Michael Nader, sexy Dex Dexter of TV's *Dynasty*, it was a nightmare in which he saw his own death that convinced him he must break the cocaine habit. Before landing his role in the super-soap series, Nader was a model who made it into movies. Already heavily into drugs, he dropped out of Hollywood and went East, following in the unsteady steps of Bobby Driscoll to the New York drug scene.

He was into everything, from LSD to cocaine. He took drugs, he said, 'because my parents had divorced and I was crying out for love. Drugs helped me become accepted and liked by the crowd.'

All around him he saw his friends 'die ugly, bloated deaths through drugs'. Then one night he had a nightmare in which he saw his own birth and death. 'I watched my body decompose. That finally jolted me back to reality and sanity.' He renounced drugs and alcohol completely in 1980. After he achieved celebrity status through *Dynasty* he took to visiting hospitals and rehabilitation centres warning youngsters of the dangers of drugs.

For Ian McShane, who, like most English actors found greater fame and fortune waiting for him Stateside, the Hollywood parties with cocktails, caviar and cocaine soured. The son of a one-time Manchester United football player and star of too many ordinary British films like *Pussycat, Pussycat, I Love You* and *Yesterday's Hero*, found that moving to America paid off, even if it was only in numerous glossy TV mini-series and soaps like *Dallas*. He also embarked on a much publicized affair with *Emmanuelle* star Sylvia Kristel. His celebrity status gave him access to the Hollywood highs – and lows.

Sniffing cocaine was just normal behaviour among the people he mixed with, and he developed his own cocaine addiction to add to his years of boozing, as he described:

I've always wanted to get as stoned as quickly as possible to enjoy the evening at the end of a working day. I could never just have one glass of wine. Vodka on ice was my favourite drink. Or just vodka. And any other substance that was going around. Anything that passed my way.

But eventually there comes a time when you can't get any more stoned and still be happy. You become miserable. Waking up with a hangover was becoming harder and more disagreeable.

I was feeling miserable, even though I was happily married [to American actress Gwen Humble] and then I started asking myself what the hell I was doing.

I saw guys around my age [in their forties] dying around me from abuse, and I knew I had to quit to survive. I'd had twenty-five years of booze and using other recreational substances.

Deciding he didn't want to be the 'oldest swinger in town' he woke up one morning in 1987 with another hangover and decided he'd had enough. He gave up drinking and using drugs. Another rehabilitated star admitting he was a bad boy.

6

Brawlers, Beaters and Belters

In April of 1920, Charlie Chaplin, then sweltering through the divorce proceedings brought against him by Mildred Harris, was eating in a fashionable hotel restaurant when he came face to face with Louis B Mayer. Under normal circumstances Chaplin may well have simply thrown the eminent movie mogul a mere passing glance of recognition. As it was Chaplin threw him a challenge to a round of fisticuffs, accusing Mayer of encouraging Mildred, who was under contract to Mayer, to press for a higher divorce settlement.

Mayer fled through the lobby and then, mustering all his courage, he turned and called Chaplin, who was in hot pursuit, a pervert. Chaplin invited Mayer to land one on him, and L B promptly obliged by punching Chaplin in the face, sending him sprawling over a potted plant. Mayer then turned and walked out unscathed.

Having lived to fight another day, Mayer did – with Sam Goldwyn. Mayer was never fond of Goldwyn and one day became so enraged with him in the showers of the Hillcrest Country Club that he knocked Goldwyn into the towel cabinet. Goldwyn threatened to sue him for a million dollars, but Mayer convinced him that such a court case would cast a dim light on the entire industry.

Earlier, in 1919, Mayer came to blows with John Gilbert during the filming of *Widow by Proxy*. Gilbert felt moved by the film's story – that of a woman forced by circumstances to turn to prostitution – to state that his own mother was a whore. Mayer, upon hearing this, attacked Gilbert, screaming, 'I ought to cut your balls off!'

A similar incident occurred on the set of *The Merry Widow* in 1924. Director Erich von Stroheim told L B Mayer that the film was about whores. Mayer told him, 'I don't make pictures about whores,' to which Stroheim responded with 'All women are whores.' Mayer knocked the director to the floor and threw him out of his office.

L B didn't come off so well in another encounter he had with Gilbert in 1928. Mayer was trying to console Gilbert on the day of what should have been his wedding to Garbo, but when the bride failed to appear the forsaken groom fled to the men's room where Mayer found him crying.

'Look, Jack,' said Mayer, 'sleep with her, but don't marry her.'

Gilbert responded to this paternal advice by decking Mayer, who fell heavily, hitting his head on a tile. Wiping away the blood and finding his feet, Mayer hissed, 'I'll destroy you.' And as head of MGM, where Gilbert was under contract, Mayer had the power to bring about Gilbert's downfall.

It had long been suggested that Mayer had the sound technician tamper with the soundtrack of Gilbert's early talkie *His Glorious Night* to make him sound risible. It is true that audiences shrieked with laughter, ultimately sealing Gilbert's fate as a 'talking' actor, but that was due to the awful dialogue. Contrary to popular belief, the soundtrack was never tampered with. Mayer's power was in having the patience to wait until Gilbert's contract with Metro ran out and then refuse to sign him to another term.

In taking a slug at Mayer, Gilbert had knocked the stuffing out of his own career and, ultimately, his life.

Brawling has often been a pastime favoured by certain film

stars; normally those who happen to drink a lot as well. At a party at Ann Rutherford's home, restaurateur Stephen Crane got into a fight in the garden with actor Turnham Bey over Crane's fiancée Lana Turner.

At another party, this one held by Gloria Swanson, silent screen hero Norman Kerry got into a drunken argument with director Marshall (Mickey) Neilan. They decided to go outside and slug it out but Swanson stopped them, saying they would draw too much attention. So she locked them in a coat closet where they beat each other half to death in the dark for twenty minutes.

Gangster star and friend of real-life mobster Bugsy Siegel, George Raft had learned how to take care of himself during his younger years as a prize-fighter. Not surprisingly, he got himself into a number of violent scrapes in Hollywood. In 1933 he starred with Wallace Beery in *The Bowery*, which included a fight scene on a barge in which Beery landed the first blow. But instead of throwing a 'screen punch', Beery, as was often his habit, threw a real punch and knocked Raft out cold. When Raft came to, he flew at Beery and it was only after several punches were exchanged that they were separated by the crew.

In 1941, during the filming of *Manpower*, tension grew between Raft and co-star Edward G Robinson – they were in competition for the affections of Marlene Dietrich, besides which, Raft resented Robinson's persistent advice on how to play his part. This led to blows on the set and they had to be separated by actor Alan Hale. Photographs of the bout made the front pages.

Two years later Raft blew his top at Peter Lorre during a scene in *Background to Danger* in which Lorre and Sydney Greenstreet tie Raft up. Lorre began improvising by blowing cigarette smoke into Raft's face, laughing sardonically. The moment Raft was free, he rushed into Lorre's dressing room and decked him.

Another frequent brawler was Errol Flynn who included among his many opponents John Huston who at that time was a lieutenant making films for the army. Huston recalled the incident:

> I had just returned to Los Angeles from the Aleutians where I had been making a film, and I came across Errol Flynn at a party at David O Selznick's house. We didn't really know each other. I knew he was under contract to Warners, where I had worked. I'd just been making a documentary about *real* heroes and I wasn't in any mood to put up with actors who were only heroic on screen. Maybe Errol picked up on my mood because he said something offensive about a lady I regarded with deep affection. I told him he was a liar and he said, 'Do you want to make something of it?'
>
> I told him I would, so we walked side by side down to the garden, reached a secluded place, and we went at it. Flynn knocked me down straight away. I landed on my elbows. I got up and he knocked me down again. I landed on my elbows again.
>
> Then I began to land some good punches. Flynn was then in very good condition. He knew how to box. He cut me above the eye and broke my nose which had been broken before. I knew I was hurting him as well, in the ribs, and so he started to wrestle.
>
> The fight went on for about an hour. There was no dirty fighting either. Errol fought clean. It was dark by the time we were finished. People were turning their cars in the driveway to leave the party and caught us in their headlights. People stepped in and separated us and we both went off to hospital. The next day Errol called me to see how I was. He had broken two ribs.
>
> I never saw him again until we made *The Roots of Heaven* twelve years later.

David Niven also recalled one of Flynn's battles:

> Flynn had a dog called Arno which he loved and took on

sailing trips on his yacht. One day Arno fell overboard and drowned, and a gossip columnist called Jimmy Fidler wrote a really nauseating article claiming that Flynn had failed to rescue his poor dog. Flynn said, 'Come on, we'll get him,' and so we spent a whole evening looking for Fidler. We found him in a night club with his wife, and Flynn went straight up to him and flattened him with a single punch. Mrs Fidler retaliated by sticking a fork in Flynn's ear. She was probably the only person who ever got the better of Flynn in a fight.

Brawling was a speciality with Flynn. Like every well-known actor playing tough characters, there was always someone drunk enough to shove him in the back with the challenge, 'OK, Mr Tough Guy, let's see how tough you really are.' Clark Gable, James Cagney and Bogart developed peaceful ways of ridding themselves of these nuisances. But not Flynn. He'd gladly wade into the attack.

When Kirk Douglas became a target for a drunkard in a bar who'd seen Douglas as the boxer in *Champion*, Kirk merely slammed his hand on the bar and shouted, 'Anyone in this bar can lick me in a fight,' and the drunkard backed off.

That kind of ploy wasn't always guaranteed to work, though. Lee Marvin used to do something similar, announcing, 'I'm a coward and I bet anybody in this place can beat me'. But one evening after a day's shooting on *Sergeant Ryker* in 1963, Marvin was continually baited by a drunk until Marvin grabbed a banjo from somewhere and smashed it over the other man's head, drawing blood and knocking out his teeth.

That man should consider himself lucky that Marvin hadn't actually been in the mood for a brawl. A few too many drinks, and Lee Marvin was often ready to come out fighting, as director Sam Peckinpah found out during a party to celebrate the finish of filming on a TV special, *The Losers*. This is how Lee Marvin told it to me:

It was the last day of shooting and they didn't need us till nine o'clock that morning, so Keenan [Wynn] and me went over to the bar and had a couple there and I said, 'You know, Keenan, it's gonna be a long hot day so we'd better stop off at the drug store and buy a jug.' So we bought a jug and hid it in the dressing room and we started on it. Right?

So by eleven when they get around to us we're in a good mood. We didn't have much to do, just sit at a table or something, and when it's over I go outside and sit in the car, and Peckinpah comes out and gives me this look. I said to him, 'What's up, Sam?'

He said, 'That scene was awful, Lee. Just fucking awful.'

By then Keenan and me are pretty drunk; and they keep stealing our bottle from the dressing room, so we'd go across the street and get another jug. By 4.30 somebody says, 'They're going to wrap in about five minutes and have a big spread over at the sound stage.'

By this time Keenan and me are *really* drunk and I said, 'Well, what are we waiting for?' and we go over. We walk in and see these tables of hors d'oeuvres, and people standing round them, and then Sam Peckinpah takes a look at me and he says, 'Don't you think you ought to have something to eat?' Something to *eat*?

Wham! goes the table and thirty feet of hors d'oeuvres are on the floor. Then Sam says something else – I don't know – so I grab him and I have him up against the wall and feet are off the ground, and I said, 'Sam, I hope you know what I mean, Sam!'

Now, he's in a tough position, right? And he says, 'That's OK Lee, just forget it.' Then I let him down and from then on it's all a bit of a blur. I was told they sent for a nurse who came at me with a needle so I grabbed her by the breast and threw her down on the hors d'oeuvres. Then I got ... I don't know; they held me down and when I woke up I was in the back of a car on my way home.

So that was Sam and me. We've gone a few rounds and we're still good friends.

Anthony Quinn had a temper on him too. But he didn't need alcohol to get him fired up. Through his veins flowed a potent mixture of Mexican and Irish blood, and a little goading from the US Marine Corps was enough to have him taking them all on when he was filming *Guadalcanal Diary* in 1943. The marines were acting as extras and kept jeering at the Hollywood phoneys.

'The director told us to keep cool,' recalled Quinn, 'but then they really started getting heavy with Lloyd Nolan. I don't know if it was the Irish temper in me or the Mexican, but I leapt on to the first marine I could reach.

'Pretty soon we were throwing bayonets at each other. There was blood everywhere and in minutes the whole scene looked like Custer's Last Stand. But we made our point and they left us alone after that.'

Quinn's tough background dictated that he had to know how to take care of himself, especially when at a young age he moved from his native Mexico into an area of Los Angeles where everyone was either Irish, Mexican or black.

Said Quinn, 'With my name I could always string along with the Irish – my father was Irish and my mother Mexican. One day there was a big gang fight between the Mexicans and the Irish. I chose that day to be a Mex because I figured that they were outnumbered by the Micks. I liked to go with the underdog.

'I got the hell beat out of me and I've been a Mexican ever since.'

Some actors manage to get themselves into trouble by picking the wrong people to slug it out with – like the police! As Bruce Willis discovered the night he threw a party and the police turned up. They had received complaints from neighbours round about midnight about the nightly festivities at the home of the star of *Die Hard* and TV's *Moonlighting*.

Willis came to the front door dressed only in a pair of trousers. When one of the police asked him to quieten the party down a bit, Willis hit him in the mouth and screamed, 'Get the fuck off my property!' Which, of course, the cops had no intention of doing. They proceeded to apprehend Willis and a fellow partygoer and dragged them screaming and kicking to the squad car.

Willis told the cops, 'You'll all be walking the fucking beat soon,' and then he yelled at the neighbours, 'Which of you bastards told the police?'

Three partygoers then stormed the police car in an attempt to free Willis and the other man. The police radioed for help and very soon ten more squad cards and twenty-five officers swarmed around Willis's home while a police helicopter spotlighted on the scene with its powerful searchlight.

Willis and four men were whisked off to jail for the night and released on bail. Willis appeared in court in June 1987 and was told he could face a three-year prison sentence. When asked by a reporter how he felt about the prospect, he admitted, 'I'm shitting myself.' From the hearing, which took ninety minutes, Willis emerged visibly shaken, having been told he must wait five days before hearing if he was to go to prison or not.

There was an immediate indication that he was prepared to turn over a new leaf. 'I don't want any more of the clink,' he said. 'I've had enough to last me a lifetime.'

He was lucky not to get a prison sentence and claims that since that time he has remained sober.

'I quit drinking,' he says. 'It was a social habit that started to get in the way.'

When boozing has led to brawling, some hellraising stars, like Willis, have gone on the wagon. It wasn't that long ago that John Hurt was drinking heavily, and had been doing so for years. It was only when his drunken behaviour led to blows that he started to reform. It was at the BAFTA awards ceremony at the Grosvenor House Hotel in London in 1989 when press photographers, seeing the drunken state he was in, decided to keep close to catch the inevitable explosion on film when it came. They knew it was unavoidable: their clicking cameras and flashing bulbs were the catalyst.

Hurt was celebrating an award which had been won by his TV series *The Storyteller* and was staggering around in a drunken haze when he turned on the paparazzi and yelled, 'Those bastards have been winding me up all night. They are all fucking hyenas and I'm going to get them.'

The other guests were stunned into silence as he began swinging into the gaggle of giggling photographers. He crashed into a table and landed heavily on the floor and had to be helped to his feet by friends. He was led away distraught and in tears.

But there were no long-lasting hard feelings between John and the press. Later that evening, as a friendly policeman escorted Hurt from the hotel, the photographers lined up and apologized to him.

'You are a wicked lot,' Hurt admonished them.

Usually when a well-deserving photographer has a punch thrown at him by a celebrity, nobody bats an eyelid – unless the fist belongs to Sean Penn – indeed everybody used to *expect* Sinatra to take a swing. A little hellraising is good for publicity. However, there are some on the receiving end of a star fist who become members of a sad sisterly fraternity – beaten wives and girlfriends. Anthony Quinn's Mexican/Irish temper got the better of him on the day he married Katherine De Mille, daughter of the director Cecil B De Mille. He flew into a rage on their wedding night when he discovered that his bride was no virgin. He hit her round the face.

'I felt betrayed,' said Quinn, 'when I discovered I wasn't the first man. The poor frightened girl packed her things and ran out, saying she was going to Reno for a divorce. After an hour I realized that if I didn't go after her, I'd never be a man.'

Katherine came back and their marriage lasted twenty-nine years, to end in 1963 when Quinn admitted he was the father of a son born to an Italian girl. Katherine divorced him and he married the Italian girl, Yolanda.

In the seventies James Caan was one of Hollywood's few major stars with pulling power on the audiences. He also packed a mean punch, according to his estranged wife Sheila. She and Caan had been separated for three years. She had custody of their three-year-old son Scott. The boy would spend a few weeks at a time with his father and when Sheila one day came to collect Scott, she mentioned that she felt she might well marry again.

According to Sheila, Caan was enraged and charged at her. 'I fell on the bed to try to protect myself,' she said. 'He struck me repeatedly on my head and my arms. I have no exact idea how many times he hit me, but it must surely have been six or more.

Sheila alleged that she was dazed for three days following the attack, suffering a black eye and a cut on her forehead. She brought an assault action against Caan but later dropped the charge. The court however issued an order banning Caan from going near her home or 'harassing, molesting or disturbing' her in any way.

Another top star of the seventies, David Soul, beat up his wife. He was then a major TV heart throb as one half of the super-cop duo in *Starsky and Hutch*. But following the close of the series, Soul, like his police partner Paul Michael Glaser, found it difficult to break away from his TV cop image. He found solace in a bottle and unleashed a terrifying temper on his wife Patti.

For two years after they married, she put up with his violent temper which once led him to throw her across the lawn and punch her, breaking bones in her hand and finger. In October 1982 she finally called the police after he slapped her across the mouth, cutting her lip.

Soul was arrested on a charge of assault and spousal abuse and led away in handcuffs. The judge ordered him to undergo a two-year programme of treatment to overcome both his booze and his violent temper problems. But the treatment had little effect, and finally Patti, unable to stand any more of his rages, divorced him.

After that David Soul went on the wagon and, according to his friend and publicist Robert Palmer, 'The erratic behaviour that led to the difficulties he had with his last wife is long gone. David has mellowed and quietened down a great deal. He quietly looked into solving his problems, he got some treatment and really has come a long way. He's proved he can cope.'

Another TV cop who's been accused of wife-beating is Larry Wilcox of *Chips*. He and his wife, Hannie, were living apart when, she said, he attacked her during an argument over financial support. According to her, he 'physically beat, then struck and assaulted' her in front of their year-old daughter. He was subsequently ordered by a court not to go within a hundred yards of her.

A-Team star George Peppard's second wife, actress Elizabeth Ashley – whom he met and fell in love with when they made *The Carpetbaggers* in 1964 – claimed that he assaulted her and came at her with a hot frying pan, an allegation that Peppard has always strongly denied.

'It caught me right on the side of my face,' she said. 'He was totally out of control.'

Peppard and Elizabeth Ashley eventually divorced, then remarried and redivorced again.

During the Swinging Sixties, *Laugh In*'s Judy Carne regularly begged 'Sock it to me'. During her three-year stormy marriage to Burt Reynolds he did, she claimed. 'At first he would get angry and only push me around. Next, he started slapping me and then finally actually punching me. In the last eight months of the marriage, he couldn't control his temper. I started to walk on eggshells for fear of setting him off.'

On rare occasions the tables are totally reversed and the husband becomes the abused. This happened to Hollywood hellraising hunk Nick Nolte who shot to fame in the TV mini-series *Rich Man, Poor Man*. His second wife was a volatile Lebanese dancer. Together they drank and sniffed cocaine, and fought. During one fiery bout she ripped the telephone out of the wall and smashed it over his head. Then she threw all his clothes into the swimming pool, and then pushed him in as well.

It was a marriage and a lifestyle that almost destroyed him. By 1984 the Hollywood hunk had turned into a bloated bulk. His face looked like it was continously hungover. His friends were bikers who roared around the freeways of California. But now, as in all good rehabilitated hellraiser stories, the only coke he touches comes from a bottle and he has a wife, Becky, who has helped him overcome the demon drink and restored him to his former hunky self.

Some married couples seem to endure, maybe even enjoy, marital brawls. There is a story about a dinner party thrown (in every sense of the word) by George C Scott and his wife Trish Van Devere which, as one guest put it, 'erupted like World War Three'.

The trouble, it seems, was political. Trish voiced her support for the vice-presidential campaign of Gerlandine Ferraro. Scott denounced the lady candidate in no uncertain terms, and the ensuing battle, which would have delighted the subject of Scott's most famous portrayal, General Patton, ended only with the timely arrival of the police.

According to the policeman called to the house, 'The kitchen table was overturned. Broken glass and dishes were all over the floor mixed with what had been served for dinner – steak, corn and potatoes. Mrs Scott had a red swollen bruise on her face, just above her right eye. Mr Scott had scratches on his forehead. He was shouting obscenities at her.'

Perhaps the most famous married marauders of the movies were Humphrey Bogart and Mayo Methot, his third wife. Lloyd Bridges, who knew Bogie, told me, 'They were known as "The Battling Bogarts". I found out why. He would invite me over for dinner quite often, and nearly every time they'd have a fight.

'It was crazy. He'd drink a little. She'd give him more, and when he'd had enough she would say something to really provoke him. So he'd hit her. That's what she seemed to *want*. I figured she must have been a masochist. It was very embarrassing.'

Another witness to the Bogart battles was David Niven.

I think that often it was jealousy – mixed with booze – that made for a lethal cocktail, with Bogie as the stirrer. They would drink and then her jealousy, usually over his current leading lady whoever it might be, would come to the boil and Bogie would goad her until the bottles were whizzing past his head.

But Mayo was sometimes Bogie's ally. One night at La Maze, a restaurant on the Strip, Bogie was confronted by a large man. I was sitting in a corner with Ann Sheridan, just a few tables away from Bogie and Mayo. We couldn't hear what was being said but the large man was bending over Bogie's table and poking him in the chest. Bogie was very cool and returning insults with a smile while Mayo was rising in anger and waiters were circling warily around taking up action stations.

Suddenly Bogie threw a full glass of scotch into the man's face while simultaneously Mayo hit the man on the head with her shoe. The large man's friends rose from their table and the waiters formed themselves into a solid phalanx, and all hell broke loose.

Ann suggested we get under the table and I wasn't about to argue but the table was too small so we crawled on hands and knees to hide under a larger table. Soon after Bogie joined us and I asked him what was going on. He said, 'Everything's OK. Mayo's handling it.' And Mayo did handle it. She ousted the large man and his friends, and the evening returned to normal.

During the sixties people with little brain were laughing at Jerry Lewis as *The Nutty Professor* and *Cinderfella*. Since he had split from his screen partner Dean Martin, he had managed to stay popular, playing dumbos with squeaky voices. His six sons, by first wife Patti, didn't find much to laugh about at home. Youngest son Joe made some dramatic accusations that his dad terrified them all with his violent behaviour.

In a *Sunday* magazine article published in 1989 Joe Lewis said his dad often 'flew into an uncontrollable rage'. For much of the time Lewis was away from his family making films. He returned home only for a week or so each month and spent most of his time in his bathroom, which contained a colour television, telephones and a fully stocked cocktail bar. The room was off-limits to the children. After Lewis left Patti for SanDee Pitnick, the boys discovered that the bathroom also contained equipment for bugging the whole house: from within the bathroom, Jerry Lewis listened in on what his sons and wife were saying.

Despite the happy family photos that appeared in the fan magazines, childhood days were miserable days for Joe who said that his dad never held him in his lap and read him stories or took him to ball games. The emotional trauma suffered by Joe and his brothers was outweighed only by the physical pain Joe claimed his father inflicted upon them, whipping and even punching them. Joe cited a time when he was four years old and playing at grocery stores with his nine-year-old brother Anthony in the kitchen. Anthony accidentally dropped a tin on his foot and Dad came raging in, grabbed Anthony and dragged him to where 'the Strap' hung. The Strap was a thick leather belt, about 3 inches wide, which hung on a hook. Pulling down Anthony's pants, Jerry Lewis whipped the boy about twenty times. 'How many more do you want?' Lewis shouted. 'Not many more,' cried the boy. Lewis beat him a further ten times, claimed Joe, who was so scared that he wet his pants.

Another time Joe heard his adopted teenage brother Ron being slammed against a wall. When Ron came into Joe's room, his white shirt was ripped and bloody, and there was blood dripping from his mouth.

All Joe's life he'd been asked what it was like being Jerry Lewis's kid and his answer was always: 'It's great, he's great'. He was never able to reveal that his life was pure hell.

Ryan O'Neal's son, Griffin, has also related tales of violent encounters with his dad, saying, 'There has been quite an exchange between me and my dad – literally. A few years ago he punched me and knocked my front teeth out. It got rid of the space between my teeth, which I didn't like anyway, so some good maybe came out of it after all.'

Griffin, however, seems to have been more of a rogue than his dad ever was. As a child he was kicked out of school for various incidents, including throwing a desk at a teacher when he was just nine years old. When he was seventeen he lost his driving licence after receiving 27 speeding summonses. He spent three days in jail after smashing up an apartment, and has done time in a drug rehabilitation centre.

He was blamed for causing the death of his friend Gian-Carlo, son of director Francis Ford Coppola, in a boating accident in 1986, and ordered to do 400 hours' community service. When Griffin failed to complete his sentence, he was put in jail for 18 days.

One of the most unusual cases of assault to come out of Hollywood in recent times was the allegation brought by manager Marie Pastor against *The Karate Kid* star Ralph Macchio. As the woman who discovered and consequently managed the karate kicking teen-idol, she told an amazing story which twenty-eight-year-old Macchio has emphatically denied.

According to Marie Pastor, Macchio was torn between his girlfriend, Phyllis, who became his wife, and his career. Pastor was, she said, having a business meeting with Macchio, who wanted to end the meeting and call Phyllis. Pastor told him that business was more important and he threw a tantrum. Then the phone rang and he began screaming at her, 'Get out of here, get out of here! She needs me!' Then he pinned her against the wall, took up a karate stance and began punching her in the breast and armpit.

A few days later while driving him home, she asked him why he'd hit her and, she alleged, 'He went crazy again, punching me so I nearly lost control of the car.'

She made these allegations in a lawsuit against Macchio, charging him with physical abuse and breach of contract. But, according to Macchio's lawyer, Norman Oberstein, 'It's so absurd and strains one's imagination. In my opinion, these charges are an attempt to retaliate for Mr Macchio having filed his own action to terminate their professional relationship.'

At the time of writing, ex-manager and Karate Kid have yet to slug it out in court.

7

Tinsel Town's Terrible Tempers

When director Elliot Silverstein was told that the role of Kid Shelleen in his up-and-coming comedy western *Cat Ballou* was to be offered to Kirk Douglas, the director turned a whiter shade of pale. *Kirk Douglas?* The actor-turned-producer who, by this time, in 1966, was notorious for being difficult on the set? The prospect filled Silverstein with horror. But the film's producer was a buddy of Douglas, and he wanted old dimple chin to play the drunken gunslinger opposite Jane Fonda as Cat.

Silverstein was given the task of approaching Douglas in an effort to entice him into accepting the part. The director had a lot of respect for Douglas as an actor but since this was to be Silverstein's first theatrical film he didn't want to have to find himself dealing with 'A consummate ego', as he put it, and then added, 'no, *huge* ego'.

Silverstein called Douglas, who had already read the script, and to Silverstein's tremendous relief, Kirk said that the part wasn't big enough for him as a star, and not small enough for a cameo.

Silverstein immediately thought, 'I'm off the hook'. He made the effort to convince Kirk that the role could be expanded, but nothing could persuade Douglas the role was worthy of him.

The director duly reported back to base camp that Douglas had rejected every concession he had made in order to get him to accept the part. When the studio chiefs asked Silverstein who he thought would be ideal for the role, Silverstein told them – Lee Marvin. It was fortunate for Silverstein that Marvin, knowing this was the film that would – and indeed did – make him a superstar, behaved impeccably throughout. But it was to Kirk Douglas's detriment that he was considered by the director to be a temperamental actor whom he didn't want to have to cope with on the set.

Kirk Douglas's reputation for being difficult has, in recent years, become something of a joke, even for those who have been on the receiving end of his temperament. At a huge Hollywood party given in his honour in 1983, his screen sparring partner Burt Lancaster announced, 'I've worked with him many times over the span of years, and I think I know him pretty well. Let me start by telling you something about him. To begin with, he is the most difficult and exasperating man that I know – except for myself.'

No wonder Sheilah Graham, the Hollywood gossip columnist, tagged Douglas and Lancaster 'The Terrible-Tempered Twins'. On their first film together, *I Walk Alone*, in 1947. they both complained to their producer Hal B Wallis, who had them under contract, that they hated their roles, and that they were grossly underpaid.

As Lancaster put it, 'We both came from sort of humble beginnings, were both young, brash, cocky, arrogant. We knew everything, were highly opinionated. We were invincible. Nobody liked us.'

From an early point in his career, Kirk Douglas tried to assert his own authority on the films he made. King Vidor, who directed him in *Man Without a Star* in 1955, said, 'I felt throughout the filming that Kirk was working himself up to being a director. This sometimes causes minor conflicts since the director has probably planned the scene weeks before and is not usually in the mood to make last-minute changes.'

So Douglas turned producer with his very next film, *The Indian Fighter*. Not long after, he was teamed up with his terrible tempered twin in *Gunfight at the OK Corral* for director John Sturges. The two stars came into the picture with their tongues firmly in their cheeks, determined to wring every moment of fun out of the script. Sturges, however, according to producer Hal B Wallis, 'ensured that no word of the original script was changed'.

Sparks flew on the set of *Strangers When We Meet* in 1960 when Douglas replaced Glenn Ford who refused to work with leading lady Kim Novak who had something of a reputation herself for being difficult. Kirk came into the project not just as actor, having ensured that his own production company, Bryna, would co-produce with director Richard Quine's own production company. And with Quine apparently attracted to Miss Novak, the scene was set for some off-screen highlights.

Douglas tried to change the script. Novak tried to stop him. She saw his attempts to wish his own brand of authority on to the production as little more than temperamental interference, and, in turn, told him how he should play his scenes.

Following this unhappy enterprise, Douglas began producing the biggest picture of his career, *Spartacus*, which Anthony Mann was set to direct. Douglas didn't want him as director but Mann was under contract to Universal who were financing the film and insisted on him. According to Douglas. 'After the first week Universal said, "Kirk, you were right. *You've* got to get rid of him." So *I* had to tell Anthony, who was a very nice guy, that we had to get somebody else.'

That somebody else was Stanley Kubrick, the young director Kirk had worked with a couple of years earlier on *Paths of Glory* and a man whose greatest success (*2001: A Space Oddysey*) and biggest disaster (*Barry Lyndon*) were the result of his mammoth ego. This second collaboration with Kirk Douglas and *his* ego turned out to be an on-set nightmare. Since 1960 Kubrick has virtually disowned the film, claiming that he was not given enough creative control. However, Douglas refutes Kubrick's claims:

> Kubrick was working for one year with Marlon Brando on *One-Eyed Jacks* while I was preparing *Spartacus*. I had worked a long time on the script with Dalton Trumbo and we worked very hard getting the right cast.
>
> I showed Kubrick the script of *Spartacus*. He said, 'I'd love to do it', and the next week I brought him over and introduced him to the cast and he started.
>
> We had many discussion with Trumbo about the script, and Stanley was in on everything. But when he came into the picture it had been cast and the script had been done, and he *did* bring about a lot of changes.
>
> All this is by way of saying the ego of film makers is a very frustrating thing. It's hard for any person to say, 'It's *my* picture. *I* did it all.'
>
> I thought Stanley did a brilliant job directing *Spartacus*. He made a *lot* of changes. The whole concept of the love scene at the beginning was originally a dialogue scene. But all the dialogue was taken out and it was done visually. And that was Kubrick's concept. It was brilliant and I'm the first to say it.

Kubrick was also responsible for casting Jean Simmons in the film when it became apparent that the actress originally chosen was inadequate. In Douglas's defence, Jean Simmons once told me, 'When Stanley came on he said he would like me to do it, and Kirk seemed to be happy about that.'

Tony Curtis, who was among the star-studded cast, also spoke in Douglas's defence. 'They held a line on Stanley a lot – Kirk, Eddie Lewis [the producer] and Universal. But Stanley in his own inimitable manner was able to say, "No, I don't like that. I'd like to try this." And he'd get it his way. But it wasn't an easy task because he was dealing with Kirk who was running the company and wanted to make sure the picture was made on his terms because he had a lot at stake.

But Stanley, I think, gave that film a style it wouldn't have had if someone else had directed it.'

Not everyone connected with the film, however, was pro-Douglas. Charles Laughton in one of his last screen performances, and one of his best, almost walked off the picture, refusing to continue working while Douglas, as he saw it, collaborated with Laurence Olivier to somehow undermine Laughton's role. Olivier had in fact been making casual suggestions to Douglas as to how his role could be improved and Douglas, in awe of Olivier, allowed the knighted actor to write his own lines.

When Laughton caught on to what was going on, he became paranoid and refused to work. It was Peter Ustinov, who shared a number of key scenes with Laughton, who persuaded Douglas to allow him and Laughton to rewrite their own scenes, thus placating the larger-than-life Laughton.

This certainly was a film of collaboration and conflict. Second Unit Director Yakima Cannutt, the famed stunt man who had directed the chariot race in *Ben-Hur* and the battle scenes in epics like *Ivanhoe* and *El Cid*, staged sections of the enormous battle between the slave army and Roman legions towards the end of *Spartacus* His job was specifically to capture shots of the main actors, such as Tony Curtis and John Ireland, in battle. He was also supposed to shoot Douglas's close fighting shots. 'I had worked out what I thought was a good routine for him and had his personal stunt man run through the scene for him,' said Cannutt. 'When the routine finished, Kirk shook his head in disapproval.'

'This is what we'll do,' Douglas told Cannutt, and he showed his stunt man his own routine, which Cannutt was obliged to film.

When they saw the 'rushes' the following day, Kirk said to Cannutt, 'Those scenes of mine are not good. I should have had scenes like the ones you shot with Curtis and Ireland. They looked great.'

Cannutt pointedly replied. 'Curtis and Ireland *took direction*.'

Douglas's next film, *The Last Sunset*, added to his rapidly growing reputation for being difficult. Another of his own productions, this was directed by tough old boot Robert Aldrich who found Douglas 'impossible to work with'. Like Kubrick before him, he was dealing with a man who wanted to be both the star *and* the producer. Said Aldrich, 'There's no doubt that my work as a director is much better if there isn't a producer. When there's a producer you get into those inevitable conflicts of how much a sequence costs and who should be in the picture – and I don't want that noise.'

Consequently, there was much 'noise' on the set.

Even Burt Lancaster became tired of Douglas's temperament when they teamed up again in 1964 to make *Seven Days in May*. Again this was in part a Kirk Douglas production and neither director John Frankenheimer nor Burt Lancaster appreciated Douglas trying to direct every scene himself, leading to arguments between the star-producer and the director. Frankenheimer believed Douglas was jealous of Lancaster. 'Kirk wanted to be Burt Lancaster – he's wanted to be Burt Lancaster all his life,' he said.

Even Lancaster found his patience strained when Douglas told him how to play his part. By this time in his life and career Lancaster's temperament had cooled considerably while Douglas's was hotter than ever. Lancaster only just tolerated Douglas's interference, partly for old time's sake and partly because Lancaster admired Kirk for daring to slight Hollywood's conservatives by openly using blacklisted screenwriter Dalton Trumbo on *Spartacus*.

Suddenly Douglas seemed to start cooling off, possibly because that last experience nearly ended his friendship with Lancaster. But Kirk's reputation went ahead of him for a few years to come. Director Andrew V McLaglen, who directed him in *The Way West* in 1967 and who is no easy pushover for any temperamental actor, told me:

It's a funny thing but I remember gritting myself for Kirk for about two months because of his reputation for being difficult. I was wondering what kind of problems I'd come up against, having heard how impossible he was to be directed.

We also had Robert Mitchum and Richard Widmark in the cast, but I knew I'd have no problems with them. When I met Kirk and started to work with him, I sort of felt I'd known him in some other life. It was a funny feeling to meet someone like that and feel that way. And I found out he wasn't difficult at all. Not with me anyway. We got on famously.

In recent years Dustin Hoffman has succeeded Kirk Douglas as an actor other actors and directors are wary of. He has also become one of the finest actors in movies. But he seems to enjoy working in an atmosphere of tension. Larry Gelbart, co-writer of *Tootsie*, when asked what he had learned from the experience of working with Hoffman, replied, 'Never to work with an actor who is smaller than the Oscar statuette!'

Even Laurence Olivier lost patience with Hoffman during the making of *Marathon Man*. The younger actor wanted to rehearse one particular gruelling scene over and over which the ailing Olivier endured until, too ill to go on, he had to give up, complaining, 'Why can't the boy just act? Why does he have to go through all this *Sturm und Drang*?'

Another of the recent 'difficult' actors is Mickey Rourke, the tough, abrasive, good-looking actor who wasn't his usual handsome self as *Johnny Handsome* (1990), in which he played a horribly disfigured hood. But it was a role he very nearly didn't get when the film's backers decided he had become too difficult to handle. Rourke only got the part because the film's director, Walter Hill, insisted on using him.

Rourke, who has been making films since Spielberg's *1941* in 1979, earned his reputation in 1987 after slamming the producers of *A Prayer For the Dying* for turning his part into 'an Irish Rambo'. He complained that he had not played the role that way, and that it had been tampered with in the editing for the sake of box office. He complained publicly, and the word was out that Rourke was turning difficult.

Then, in 1989, he caused a storm over *Wild Orchid*, refusing to promote the film when *Playboy* published pictures of himself and his on-screen/off-screen lover Carre Otis in explicit moments from the film. It was reported that the couple had made love for real, and that the scene had to be drastically cut by the censors. He was also blamed for breaking co-star Paul Land's ribs when, it was claimed, Rourke insisted on realism in a fight scene he had with Land.

Hollywood has always had difficult actors to cope with. Wallace Beery, one of the most beloved (by the public) actors of the silent screen and early talkies, often antagonized the people he worked with. While making *Slave Ship* in 1937, he had to slap cabin boy Mickey Rooney around. But he slapped him so hard that blood trickled down Rooney's face. Director Tay Garnett took Beery aside and pointed out that Rooney was loved by everyone on the set as well as at the studio, and it would be 'most unfortunate if someone decided to part your hair with a sun arc. So stop slapping the boy around.'

During the filming of another sea-going saga, *Mutiny on the Bounty* (1935 version), Charles Laughton upstaged Gable, who complained to director Frank Lloyd, 'Laughton's treating me like an extra. He didn't even look at me when he addressed me. The audience won't see me in the sequence. Laughton hogged it.' Gable refused to work further and Metro's boy-wonder Irving Thalberg had to fly out to the location at Catalina to calm Gable down and persuade him to continue filming.

Gable lost his cool with his pal Spencer Tracy who often tested the patience of his peers. During Tracy's death scene in *Test Pilot* (1938), Tracy lay in Gable's arms dying 'the slowest, most lingering death in history', as Gable described it. Again and again, Tracy upstaged Gable by returning from the point of death with a weak smile until Gable finally dropped Tracy and yelled, 'Die, goddammit, Spence! I wish to Christ you would!'

Some actors succeeded in getting everyone to hate them. William Wellman, who directed *Beau Geste* in 1939, said of Brian Donlevy, who played the sadistic sergeant in that film, 'I've never seen a guy that could completely get everybody to dislike him as he could.'

Donlevy 'lorded it over everybody else' and exasperated Ray Milland so much that during a fencing sequence, Milland aimed for an unpadded spot on Donlevy, managing to draw blood. Donlevy fainted and the crew applauded.

It's probably true to say that some actors just don't mix well with other actors or directors. This would seem true of Richard Widmark who gave no trouble to McLaglen but, according to Pilar Wayne ('the Duke's' third and last wife) proved difficult during the making of Wayne's beloved (and still much underrated) *The Alamo* in 1960. Widmark had recently joined John Ford's repertory company and so Wayne, who was producing and directing as well as starring as Davy Crockett, was delighted when Widmark accepted the role of Jim Dowie – so much so that he took an ad in the *Hollywood Reporter* reading 'Welcome aboard, Dick.'

When 'Dick' met Wayne for the first time, Widmark said to the Duke, 'Tell your press agent that the name is *Richard.*'

Struggling to control his temper (he could probably have flattened his co-star), Wayne replied 'If I ever take another ad, I'll remember that, *Richard.*'

From the very beginning of filming on location in Bracketville, Widmark challenged Wayne's authority. When Widmark began questioning Wayne's direction, Big John responded initially with patience and understanding because he greatly respected and admired the other actor. But Widmark seemed to see this as a sign of weakness and continued to argue with Wayne in front of the cast and crew. Eventually Wayne's patience ran out and in a violent confrontation, Wayne finally threw the smaller Widmark against a wall. There was less arguing after that, but the two actors never became bosom buddies and never worked together again.

A couple of years earlier Wayne had come into conflict with director John Huston when they made *The Barbarian and the Geisha* in 1957. It was a picture which Wayne believed would finally stretch him as an actor. But his method of filming and Huston's were worlds apart. Wayne wrote from the location in Japan to his wife Pilar back home, 'I can't work with the son-of-a-bitch.' He complained that whenever he asked Huston what tomorrow's shooting schedule was, the director would simply reply, 'Spend more time absorbing the beauty of the scenery and less time worrying about your part.' Then Wayne would complain that he couldn't memorize the next day's dialogue if he didn't know what they were filming, and Huston, according to Wayne, replied, 'Don't worry, we'll improvise.'

Wayne told Pilar, 'The son-of-a-bitch can't make a good movie without his father or Bogart to carry him.'

Huston, however, told me that he had been persuaded to accept the job of directing the film before the script had been completed.

It might have been a better picture. It *was* a good picture before it became a bad picture. When we returned from Japan to Hollywood, it was all finished. As far as I was concerned it was a sensitive, well-balanced work. I turned it over to the studio and went to work on *The Roots of Heaven*, and apparently John Wayne took over after I left. He pulled a lot of weight at Fox, so they went along with his demand for changes. He had a number of scenes reshot because he didn't like the way he looked in the original scenes, and by the time he had finished hacking up the picture, it was a complete mess.

Actors from either side of the Atlantic have often found themselves at loggerheads. Kenneth More told me of the unfortunate happenings on the set of *The Mercenaries* which he made in 1966 in Jamaica with Hollywood star (though

Australian born) Rod Taylor and American football star Jim Brown.

Rod Taylor proudly told me, 'I had Johnny Mills in my last film.' Most people would have said, 'I have been filming with Johnny Mills.' I had a feeling he would tell the cast of his next film, 'I had Kenny More in my last film.' He was the *star*, and I was billed below Yvette Mimieux and American football player Jim Brown. I just felt like I didn't belong with them.

If Rod or Jim weren't on the set on time, we would have to wait about until they arrived. Sometimes we didn't get started until 10 o'clock, which is a late start on a film. It was all so undisciplined. They thought they were such big stars, but they just created tension.

Taylor had been an amateur boxer and Jim of course was a former American football player and was a big man, and he and Taylor kept threatening to settle their disputes with their fists. They appeared to hate each other. If they were only acting, then they were better actors than I thought.

They all put in their tenpenny's worth about what they thought should be filmed, but nobody asked my opinion, and I'd been in more films than the rest of the cast put together. Director Jack Cardiff cut all my best lines in deference to the Hollywood stars. I'd wake up in the mornings, unable to face another day on that film.

Richard Harris has had his fair share of feuds with Hollywood actors, although it isn't always easy to disinguish exactly who is the heavy in his conflicts. He reported that Marlon Brando refused to play scenes with him during the shooting of *Mutiny on the Bounty*, although it's never been quite clear if this story isn't perhaps just a bit of blarney from the Irish hellraiser. The tale he told journalist Gerard Garrett was that Brando wouldn't hit him hard enough in a scene for it to look real. After the third take and the third feeble blow,

Harris taunted him with 'Shall we dance?' Brando refused to act with him in the end and Harris found himself addressing his lines not to Brando but a packing case acting as a stand-in.

It's a good story but Harris is clearly seen in shot with Brando during the final scene of the film – Christian's death scene – which was the last shot to be filmed. (It's also odd that at no time during the film is Brando seen to strike Harris anyway!)

Harris has been known to cause a few directors to have sleepless nights. In his own defence Harris told Garrett, 'I ring up a director at 2 o'clock in the morning to discuss a scene. I turn up on the set with twenty pages of notes. I say this is true co-operation.'

Harris didn't get on with Kirk Douglas when they made *The Heroes of Telemark* in 1965 (but then at that time few got on with Douglas), and just a year earlier he crossed swords with Mr Epic himself, Charlton Heston, on the set of *Major Dundee* in Mexico. It was a troubled film, directed by Sam Peckinpah who constantly had the Columbia Studio brass breathing down his neck. Heston, who had director, script and cast approval, bought Peckinpah extra filming time by returning his salary to the studio, convinced they wouldn't accept it. They did. And while all this brouhaha was going on Richard Harris was getting up Heston's famously broken nose.

Harris, Heston claimed, may appear to be very strong, but he 'does seem to be one of those people who seemed to enjoy ill health. In any event, on this picture, he was from time to time spectacularly taken with a seizure of one kind or another.'

Said Heston, 'Richard is very much the *professional Irishman*. I found him a somewhat erratic personality and an occasional pain in the ass.'

Harris fell foul of Heston's neurosis about actors who arrive late on the set, and found himself being reprimanded by the man who personified Moses to most moviegoers. To Harris, however, he was simply another actor and, unimpressed, the Irish actor said:

Heston's the only man who could drop out of a cubic moon – he's so square [very hip talk for 1964!]. We never got on. The trouble with him is he doesn't think he's just a hired actor like the rest of us. He thinks he's the entire production. He used to sit there in the mornings and clock us in with a stop-watch.

I got sick of this, so I brought an old alarm clock and hung it around my neck and set it to go off at the moment he walked in one day.

He said, 'I don't find that amusing,' and I said, 'Well, you know what you can do, don't you.'

Richard Harris, according to Heston, was 'something of a fuck-up', but conceded, 'However, if he was a fuck-up, I was a hard-nosed son of a bitch.'

Another British actor who ran foul of Heston's time-keeping neurosis was Maxwell Caulfield, who played Heston's totally unlovable son in the *Dynasty* spin-off *The Colbys*. Again Heston held a good deal of creative control over the enterprise, and made his point to Caulfield by writing him a firm letter telling him to be on time or else.

Caulfield failed to endear himself to his screen mother, Stephanie Beacham, in the early stages of filming the series. Caulfield was passing by Stephanie's dressing room with a friend and, pointing to the glamorous actress, said, '*That*, in there, is supposed to be my mother.'

Stephanie, who on screen proved she was Queen Bitch, turned on Caulfield, sharpened her acting talons and told him, 'Not only am I going to prove in front of the camera that I *am* your mother, but I'm also the person who will knock you into *shape*.'

He was, she said 'such a hothead when he entered the series. He calmed down, mainly because of his lovely wife Juliet Mills.'

Some actors just seem to have a knack for making themselves unpopular. King Yul Brynner reached a stage in his career where he seemed to feel he was holding court over

all else about him, whether British or American. During the
making of *The Magnificent Seven* Steve McQueen didn't get on
with him at all, and neither did any of the British actors in *The
Long Duel*. On location in Spain in 1966, he tested the
patience of the rest of the cast with his boasting, as Patrick
Newell remembered.

> One day, while we were sitting around having some
> coffee with a few other actors, he suddenly said, 'Of
> course *The Magnificent Seven* would have been nothing
> without me.' And everyone was muttering names like
> Charles Bronson, Steve McQueen and James Coburn. I
> mean, the line-up in the film was terrific, but as far as Yul
> Brynner was concerned there would have been no film
> without him.
>
> And then we used to play games with him and we were
> going to invent a game that didn't exist because whatever
> you said, Mr Brynner always said, 'Well, as a matter of
> fact I was world champion pistol shot,' or 'I'm the world
> champion' of whatever it was you mentioned. So we were
> going to make up a sport to see what he said, and in Spain
> they play a game called callots. So someone suddenly
> said, 'There's a really terrific game going on in the square
> in Granada,' and we were just waiting and then Brynner
> said, 'Of course, I'm the South American callot
> champion.'
>
> I remember Trevor [Howard] just standing up and
> looking at him, mouthing a bad word and walking out of
> the room.
>
> After we returned to Pinewood Studios there was a
> knock at my dressing room door one day, and Trevor
> came in and said, 'Come to my dressing room.' I said,
> 'Why?' and he said, 'Just come into my room.'
>
> I went into his room and it was pitch dark. He said,
> 'Have you seen outside?'
>
> And I looked out and there was this enormous caravan
> parked outside, closing off the light through Trevor's

window. He said, 'Give you one guess whose that is,' and I said, 'It's Mr Brynner's,' and he said, 'Yes, it is.'

There was this veranda on the back of the caravan which Yul Brynner had got from somewhere, and he was sitting on this veranda in his black shirt, black boots and black trousers and smoking a big cigar. And Trevor said, 'That bastard! We'll see about this.'

So we went out and Trevor said, 'Morning, amigo. Lovely caravan. *Quite* big.'

Brynner said, 'It's the *biggest* in the whole world.' And Trevor just turned round and gave it this tremendous kick. There was a loud *Boing!* and Trevor didn't say any more to him but just went back and called the first assistant director and said, 'I want that monstrosity out of my window.'

There were some serious incidents involving Yul Brynner, to do with embarrassing girls. One day, for instance, a female journalist came on the set to interview Brynner who proceeded to make her look pretty stupid in front of everybody on the set. I thought Trevor was actually going to hit him, but the first assistant came over and courageously tore a strip off Brynner. That was the sort of thing that turned Trevor red with fury. Eventually he wouldn't play scenes with Yul Brynner.

A more recent example of cross-Atlantic friction came on the set of *Sunset* (1989) between Bruce Willis and Malcolm McDowell. At the climax of the film McDowell, who has to be rescued from the sea by Willis, had to endure the freezing water throughout several takes because director Blake Edwards was not satisfied with Willis's performance. The two actors reputedly almost came to blows and ended the film not talking to each other.

Willis was blamed for costly delays that plagued filming throughout, and it's said that he antagonized his co-stars by constantly ad-libbing during takes, leaving the other actors speechless.

There were stories too, in 1969, about George Lazenby, who succeeded Sean Connery as James Bond for *On Her Majesty's Secret Service* (by far the best Bond movie). When Connery decided to hang up his licence to kill and super-spy toupee after five successive 007 epics, the producers Cubby Broccolli and Harry H Saltzman chose Big Fry man George Lazenby from Australia as the actor who best filled Ian Fleming's description of Commander Bond (save for the Australian accent).

Filming had barely commenced when stories began to circulate about Lazenby's 'difficult' behaviour. He was arguing with the director Peter Hunt and his co-star Diana Rigg. There were complaints from Lazenby that Diana Rigg was eating garlic before their big love scene. Diana Rigg denied the allegations.

However, Lois Maxwell, who played the ever-loyal Miss Moneypenny, says, 'Diana and I had lunch together and after eating some shrimps she realized how much garlic there had been in them. I told her to chew tea leaves to get rid of the smell, but it didn't work.'

One of the numerous girls in the film, Catherine Schell, told me that Lazenby was never difficult or temperamental. 'I never had any trouble with George. In fact we used to send him up something rotten, Angela Scoular and I. We'd make funny faces at him from behind the camera, trying to make him corpse. The poor guy really had it rough but he took it all quite well.'

The producers vowed before filming was over that Lazenby would never again work for Her Majesty's Secret Screen Service. The critics drove the final nails in the coffin by failing to recognize the film's new and exciting style (thanks to Peter Hunt who oddly never made another Bond movie) and John Barry's finest ever Bond score, concentrating their venom instead on Lazenby's 'wooden performance'. In fact, Lazenby was hardly more wooden than Connery had been in *Dr No*.

Lazenby's career took a nose dive and he turned to drink and drugs for solace. Today he is more of a celebrity than an actor, making cameo appearances, commercials and turning up at premières. But he maintained that he was never 'difficult'.

That was just bullshit made up by the producers. I was never late, I always knew my lines and, if you look at the records, I had one take on practically every shot. The crew loved me. I used to get on their case if ever there were any injustices towards anybody. That's the way I was. The hard-to-handle rumour was spread to stop me working. And it did, very successfully.

The *Hollywood Reporter* sent me a note saying it's the 25th Anniversary of James Bond, would you like to take out an ad. What for? To do what? To say thanks Cubby for what you did to me? If I wanted to kiss ass with the business, which I've never done, then that's what I'd do. But I've always been my own man and I don't bullshit.

Even the ever-amiable Roger Moore fell out with Broccolli after discovering that secret auditions to find a replacement for Moore as Bond were carried out in 1980. At the time Moore told me he would never play Bond again. After their feud hit the headlines, Broccolli ceased conducting the secret auditions and made Moore an offer he couldn't refuse to play Bond several more times.

Producers, and directors, have often been greater villains than those portrayed by actors on screen. So have many of the great Hollywood moguls and studio heads. Their jobs, by their very nature, were manipulative, and some, like Harry Cohn of Columbia, were positively loathed by many he had under contract. Cohn set up a spy system at the studio with microphones on every sound stage which were connected to a speaker in his office. He ensured that no one could talk confidentially and if he heard something he didn't like, he would loudly announce over the intercom, 'I heard that!'

The lecherous Cohn once used his intercom to address an embarrassed starlet when he asked her if she was keeping herself in a state of sexual readiness for him. Eventually, directors like George Stevens and Howard Hawks retaliated by deliberately making unflattering remarks about Cohn.

In the golden days of cinema, feuds often erupted between roguish directors and powerful studio heads. People are still wondering exactly what went on during the filming of the notorious orgy scene in Erich von Stroheim's *The Wedding March* in 1928. Shooting sometimes lasted twenty hours at a time as the extras were treated to squab, caviar and champagne. The set was closed and the extras were loyal to Stroheim's oath of silence. When the Paramount brass saw the rushes, they cut the scene drastically to comply with the Hays Office's code.

Viennese-born Stroheim never was the darling of the studios because he was so ruthlessly extravagant. His first important film *Foolish Wives* cost Universal a staggering million dollars. He spent the money on ensuring every detail was totally authentic, right down to the underwear worn (though never seen) by Austrian troops. His films were also extremely *long*. The studio's young head, Irving Thalberg, was rightly worried that *Foolish Wives* would never make a profit. It did well, in a truncated version, but had cost so much that it didn't earn the studio a profit, and consequently Thalberg fired the profligate Stroheim during the filming of *Merry-Go-Round*.

As fate would have it, Thalberg joined the newly formed MGM, which put Stroheim to work on *Greed*. Once more in conflict with Stroheim, the young boy wonder of Metro had Stroheim replaced and the film drastically cut.

In 1928 screen goddess Gloria Swanson hired Stroheim to direct her in the lavish *Queen Kelly*, but after he had wasted $600,000 on meaningless footage, Swanson fired him. After that no studio would touch him, although he made a good living as an actor and was even reunited with Gloria Swanson to recount more glorious days in *Sunset Boulevard*.

Otto Preminger – or Otto the Ogre – was another Viennese-born film director who established himself as a man

Burton and Taylor
(above left) began their
love affair on *Cleo-
patra*. It ended, due to
Burton's hellraising,
when he made *The
Clansman*. (*Twentieth
Century-Fox*)

Tony Curtis and his
wife, former model
Leslie Allen (above
right), just two months
after his drugs bust.

While many actors
loathed Otto 'The
Ogre' Preminger, at
least one person loved
him – his wife.

Humphrey Bogart, seen here with his wife Lauren Bacall, knew how to get his way on a film set – as Lee Marvin was to discover and emulate.

Lovable Hollywood rogue Lee Marvin was at the height of his hellraising career when he starred with Clint Eastwood in *Paint Your Wagon* in 1969. (*Paramount Pictures*)

Richard Dreyfuss is another top Hollywood star who faced the ups and downs of stardom through a drug-induced haze. Happily, he survived.

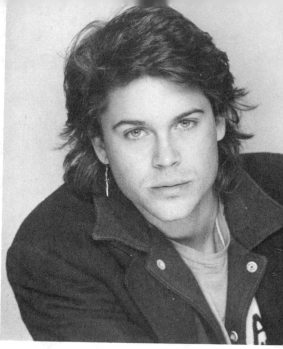

Matthew Broderick, young star of *Glory*, became a headline-making brat-packer. (*Tri-Star Pictures*)

Rob Lowe's problems were due to his addiction to women. (*Cinema Bookshop*)

Brat-packer Sean Penn (seen here in *Casualties of War*) is more famous for being a trouble-maker and Madonna's ex-husband than for any film he has made so far. (*Columbia Pictures*)

many loved to hate. After only a week of filming his third American film, *Kidnapped*, in 1937, he was fired by Darryl F Zanuck after an argument, and Zanuck saw to it that Preminger was virtually blacklisted. It was 1942 before he was allowed back at Fox to make another film – Zanuck was as that time away on war service and knew nothing about it. But when Zanuck returned and found Preminger at his studio, he promptly fired him from directing *Laura*, allowing him only to remain on the film as its producer. However, when the replacement director proved inept, Zanuck reinstated Preminger, and Otto the Ogre continued to direct – and stir up trouble – until his death in 1986.

The reputation he gained for himself was one he seemed to enjoy. He laughed when he heard that Billy Wilder had said, 'I hear Otto's on holiday. In Auschwitz.'

He knew how to upset actors and seemed to take a delight in it. Linda Darnell despised him because he had treated her so badly when making *Fallen Angel* and *Forever Amber*. Her dislike of him was such that during the filming of *A Letter to Four Wives*, in which she picks up a photograph of a man and reacts with distaste, director Joe Mankiewicz used a photo of Preminger which prompted exactly the right expression from Darnell.

When Otto directed Trevor Howard in a TV version of *Brief Encounter* restoring Noël Coward's original storyline and title of *Still Life*, Preminger told Howard, 'Forget about the picture you made. Here ve haf something different. Ve haf Ginger Rogers. You must pick her up, take her to the counter for coffee and pinch her ass.'

Howard thought for a few moments and then said, 'I think I know what time the next plane leaves for London.' He stayed, of course, but hated working for Preminger.

When Preminger once said to Howard, 'You don't like me, do you?' Howard replied, 'You know very well I don't.'

Robert Mitchum fell out with Preminger on their third and last film together, *Rosebud*, in 1975. Mitchum had arrived on the set for an early call and found they were nowhere near ready for him. According to one account, he went to the catering tent where the crew were having breakfast, and shook the centre pole fiercely, loudly claiming that this was going to cost Preminger plenty. He swooped on Preminger who rebuked him for being drunk, raging, 'You ver drunk last night and you are drunk now.'

Mitchum described the occasion. 'It was 5.30 in the morning and I tried to reason with Otto by saying how could I possibly be drunk at that time. Besides, the script called for me to look beat-up and dishevelled. But he wouldn't listen to me, so I turned and yelled "Taxi!" He replaced me with Peter O'Toole. It broke my heart. I was one of the few people who understood him.'

Temperaments and egos abound in Hollywood. Without them movies might just be flickering images, put together with some talent and no passion.

8

The Rat Pack

While Brando and Dean were rebelling, and people like Peter Finch and Lee Marvin were raising hell, there was another, more exclusive, fraternity of Hollywood Rogues into which membership was purely by invitation. These men were real Rats and the leader of the Pack was one Francis Albert Sinatra. Key members were Sammy Davis Jnr, Dean Martin, Peter Lawford and Joey Bishop.

They lived by a simple code: do what the hell you liked, do it together, but be loyal to the King Rat. There lay the mistake that Peter Lawford ultimately made. And Sinatra punished him for the rest of his life. He was excommunicated from the Pack. Doomed to eternal damnation from Sinatra's own special brand of heaven.

Poor Peter Lawford's crime was to love his friend, the President, John F Kennedy, more than he loved his King.

Lawford was the son of a knighted World War One British General. Educated in private schools, young Peter made his screen début at the age of eight in a British film, *Poor Old Bill* (1931). During a visit to California in 1938, the well-spoken English child actor was given the supporting role as a Cockney lad in *Lord Jeff*. He was taken under the paternal wing of

139

MGM who launched him in 1942 in tiny roles in prestige films like *Mrs Miniver* and *Random Harvest*, finally allowing him his first major role in 1945 in *Son of Lassie*, and to blossom as a leading man opposite leading ladies such as Judy Garland (*Easter Parade*), June Allyson (*Two Sisters from Boston*), and Elizabeth Taylor (*Little Women*).

It was in 1947 that he appeared in *It Happened in Brooklyn*, playing second fiddle to a scrawny thirty-one-year-old bobby-sox idol with hollow cheeks, Frank Sinatra. Sinatra, dubbed 'The Voice', was enjoying enormous popularity on radio, in nightclubs and now in films. There was something about the elegant fist-fighting, swearing, tough little New York-born Italian son-of-a-gun that appealed to the ever-so-ever-so English son of a knight. Sinatra had friends in low places. His Italian blood attracted him to the most powerful Latins in America, and nobody who knew about his Mafioso connections messed with him. He could be brash, cocky and arrogant. Even as a newcomer to films, after his first MGM picture, *Anchors Aweigh* (1945), he told a reporter 'Hollywood stinks!'

By the time he came to work with Lawford, Sinatra's reputation for roughing it with the press was already growing. His love-hate relationship with reporters made headlines, especially when he came to blows with a columnist in a nightclub.

But as his much publicized marriage to Ava Gardner deteriorated, so too did his friendship with Lawford. MGM had opposed Sinatra's pursuit of Ava, also under contract to Metro, and he had opposed Louis B Mayer's pursuit of poor star vehicles for him. Against his studio's advice, he and Ava married in 1951. It lasted only a year (although there was no divorce until 1957) and some time after that Peter Lawford made the mistake of meeting Ava, who'd just returned from a trip overseas, for a drink in a Hollywood restaurant.

They talked over old times. They laughed. Nearby gossip columnist Louella Parsons listened attentively. The next day her column heralded, 'Ava's first date back in the US is Peter Lawford.'

At 3 o'clock the following morning Lawford was awakened

by a phone call. Sinatra was on the other end, furious. 'What the fuck are you doing going out with Ava?' he ranted. 'You want both of your legs broken?'

'But, Frank, we just had a drink ...' Lawford tried to explain. But Sinatra wouldn't listen. He didn't speak to Lawford again for seven years. But Lawford didn't learn from his mistake.

Sinatra went through the worst period of his career when Universal signed him to a contract, put him in a disaster – *Meet Danny Wilson* (1952) – and then dropped him. His vocal chords abruptly haemorrhaged; CBS TV dropped him, as did his agent MCA, and Columbia Records with whom he had been for ten years. Suddenly everyone was prepared to write him off.

He was so desperate to work again that he begged Columbia Pictures to give him the role of Maggio in *From Here to Eternity* (1953). They told him his usual fee of $150,000 was too high. He said he'd do it for $8,000. They thought it over and only after their first choice, Eli Wallach, announced he would be doing a Broadway play instead of making the film, did they give the part to Sinatra. It earned him an Oscar as Best Supporting Actor.

He now embarked on a new recording contract for Capitol, and proved wrong all the critics who'd said he was just emulating Crosby when he developed his own new determined style which culminated in 1955 with his album *Songs For Swinging Lovers*, one of the first best-selling LPs.

His Oscar brought him further worthwhile film roles, often allowing him the chance to sing, as in *Young at Heart* and *The Joker is Wild*, but to turn in fine performances also. He was now an important singer – one of the most important – and an accomplished and sought-after actor. He was, and remains, one of the top entertainers of all time.

There was bound to be some tension when he teamed with Marlon Brando for *Guys and Dolls* in 1955. Sinatra wasn't a trained actor. He went on instinct. He liked to get on with things. Brando used the Method. After eight takes of a scene in which Sinatra had to eat cheesecake while Brando spoke, Sinatra finally lost his temper. He slammed his fork on the table, leapt up and yelled, 'These fucking New York actors! How much cheesecake do you think I can eat?' Then he stormed off the set.

During another series of takes Sinatra threatened to leave and told the director, 'When Mumbles is through rehearsing, I'll come out.'

Mankiewicz always refuted stories that Sinatra gave him a hard time on the set, but one of Mankiewicz's sons said that his father 'finished the picture hating Sinatra'. If Sinatra ever blew a line he would make 'such excuses as "There's an extra talking back there".'

Sinatra stormed off of the set of *Carousel* on the first day of shooting because it was to be shot in both the new CinemaScope 55 format and the standard 'flat' ratio, meaning everything had to be shot twice. And Sinatra wasn't going to do everything twice.

During the late fifties the Rat Pack began to come together. In 1959 Dean Martin turned up in a Sinatra film, *Some Come Running*, having been wandering in the Hollywood wilderness since breaking up with his former screen buddy Jerry Lewis. From 1948, when Hal B Wallis signed Lewis and Martin to a contract, the comedy duo had made sixteen money-spinning films, but after *Hollywood or Bust* (1956) they did bust. As they went their separate ways, critics gave Martin, who had been the straight man of the team, little chance of finding the kind of success they predicted for Lewis. At first their predictions seemed destined to come true. But once Martin had Sinatra on his side, he couldn't fail.

Sammy Davis Jnr also came to the fore thanks to Sinatra. Davis's struggle to overcome the racial prejudice that held him back was backed by Sinatra. From the age of four, Davis had been on the stage, starting out as a novelty turn in his father's vaudeville dance routine. He avoided the child-labour inspectors by clamping a cigar between his teeth and pretending he was a forty-five-year-old midget.

He was drafted into the army in 1942, where he discovered that even in uniform everyone was not as equal as God had intended. He was subjected to beatings just for being black. 'I must have had a fight every two days,' he said. 'That's why my nose ended up flat against my face.'

When the war was over Davis returned to the stage, refusing to submit to performing Al Jolson-caricatures or being the submissive Negro to the bigoted entrepreneurs. He performed in a hotel where he was not allowed to stay because blacks were barred. Then a chance meeting with Frank Sinatra changed everything, and the doors that had been closed to blacks suddenly opened for Sammy Davis Jnr.

'Frank knew all about intolerance,' said Davis. 'He'd been called a wop and I was called a coon. Before meeting him, I was just another black entertainer. He gave me the key.'

Broadway welcomed him in 1956 in *Mr Wonderful* and Hollywood beckoned. His film career started with *The Benny Goodman Story*. His nightclub act earned him a fortune, much of which he spent on whisky, marijuana and cocaine.

In the meantime, Sinatra's relationship with Peter Lawford had been repaired when they met again at a dinner party given by Gary Cooper, and they behaved as though there had never been an argument. Peter was by then married to Patricia Kennedy, sister of John F Kennedy. Sinatra became so fond of the Lawfords that he kept a special room for them at his home.

One New Year's Eve the Lawfords, along with Natalie Wood and Robert Wagner, were dining with Sinatra at his Beverly Hills mansion. They'd planned to go with Sinatra to his home in the desert to see in the New Year. But the weather took a turn for the worse and Lawford suggested that maybe they ought to wait until morning.

Sinatra flew into a rage and yelled, 'Well *I'm* going,' and he stormed out.

Everyone went home after that. The next morning the Lawfords returned to Sinatra's home and found that all their clothes, which they stored in their own special room, had been thrown into the swimming pool.

Sinatra seemed to reach a point where he thought he could do as he liked. When he didn't like the bedroom furniture in his penthouse suite at the Fontainebleau Hotel in Miami he ordered his bodyguards to throw the offending furniture out, according to his former bodyguard Andy Celentano, who said, 'One time he took a dislike to the piano. "Hey," he said, "let's toss this." So me and him struggled to throw the thing out of the window. Luckily it was too heavy to lift.'

One night they went to a Miami club. According to Celentano, the first thing Sinatra did was to throw his chair across the room, yelling, 'Get rid of this. I want a high-back chair.' The manager came over and a furious argument ensued, nearly leading to blows. Sinatra would have started a fight there and then but his minders knew that the club had its own hit men and refused to start throwing punches. He stormed out, cursing his men for backing down.

Various actors and entertainers drifted in and out of the Rat Pack. After co-starring with Sinatra in *Kings Go Forth* in 1958, Tony Curtis became a temporary member. He and his wife Janet Leigh, who was pregnant with Jamie Lee Curtis, were Rat Packing with the others at Peter Lawford's house in Santa Monica. After the party Curtis, Janet, Dean Martin and songwriter Sammy Cahn piled into a car and drove off. They were followed by another couple, David and Patricia North, with Frank Sinatra bringing up the rear. Suddenly the Norths' car was purposely rammed by a man who believed that his footloose wife was hiding in it. The attacking vehicle bounced off its target and hit Curtis's car. Janet Leigh became hysterical and began screaming. Dean Martin, Sammy Cahn and Tony tried to calm her down while Sinatra reached for his car radio and called for the police and an ambulance.

Janet Leigh was still hysterical when the ambulance arrived to take her away. Sinatra was having a field day, standing up in his car and bellowing 'Mayday! Mayday!' Police took away the crazed driver.

But Tony Curtis's membership of the Rat Pack was short-lived. He told me, 'It was terrific. I felt like a man. To be included in this circle was a wonderful feeling for me. But I didn't feel comfortable for some reason.' He handed in his membership card.

In 1960 the Rat Pack – Sinatra, Lawford, Martin, Davis and Bishop – came together to make *Ocean's Eleven*, a caper that became a classic only because it featured for the first time the nucleus of the clan. Joey Bishop, the least known of the Pack, had enjoyed a modest nightclub career as a comedian before serving in the US Army during the war. But during the fifties he too came under the patronage of Frank Sinatra, and he became a popular TV personality and starred in his own situation comedy. For a while he even hosted his own talk show.

These men, with stories of their womanizing, boozing and brawling, were dubbed the 'Rat Pack' by the press, not altogether an affectionate term. Dean Martin refuted those stories, though. 'They're just that,' he said in 1983 on the set of *The Cannonball Run II*, 'they're just stories. But we did have a lot of fun.'

No steam rooms full of naked girls?

'Hell, no, we were all married. And we always took our wives because we couldn't stand to kiss 'em goodbye.'

Well, maybe that's how Dean Martin remembers it all, but Sinatra's marriage to Ava Gardner had finished in 1952 and he didn't marry Mia Farrow until 1966. And, apart from a brief marriage much earlier, Sammy Davis Jnr remained single until his marriage in 1960 to Swedish actress May Britt. She eventually left him, unable to cope with his cocaine and alcohol abuse. As for Peter and Pat Lawford, they fixed it so that John Kennedy and Marilyn Monroe could screw around without Jackie finding out. Lawford even took photographs of the President of the United States and the blonde bombshell in bed together. Yes, the Rat Pack did have a lot of fun.

They were reunited in 1962 for *Sergeants Three*. But the clan was about to lose one of its most important members – Peter Lawford.

John Kennedy, the President of the United States, liked

Sinatra and admired his taste in women. But brother Bobby felt that Sinatra's lifestyle was damaging for the President's image. Things came to a head in March 1962 when Sinatra offered Kennedy the use of his Palm Springs home.

Bobby Kennedy, as Attorney-General, had been helming a penetrating investigation into numerous underworld figures, including Sam Giancana, a close friend of Sinatra, and another regular guest of the singer. Bobby Kennedy declared Sinatra's home a security risk, and the President had to cancel his stay at the Sinatra mansion.

Sinatra blew his top and accused both Lawfords of covering up what he saw as a vendetta being waged by Bobby against him. He never again spoke to Peter Lawford.

There were occasional Rat Pack, or semi-Rat Pack movies. Dean Martin and Frank Sinatra had more fun than the audience in the comedy western *Four for Texas* (1963), and in 1964 Bing Crosby joined Sinatra, Martin and Davis for *Robin and the Seven Hoods*. Martin and Sinatra did *Marriage on the Rocks* (1965), and the following year Dino and Joey Bishop were in the spoof western *Texas Across the River* (1966).

During the sixties Sinatra's star rose ever higher in Hollywood. He wasn't just an *actor* or even just a movie *star*. He had become a legend and he ensured he got the kind of treatment only a legend deserved. While filming *Von Ryan's Express* in Italy in 1965, he arrived each day on location by helicopter while Trevor Howard and the rest of the cast had to make the journey by car along bumpy tracks.

James Brolin, who was in the film, said:

Sinatra was sort of at his prime. One day he would say, 'Hello, Jim, how are you today?' and the next you could say 'Hi, Frank,' and he'd walk right by you. You never really knew where he was going to be at. I don't know if chemically he'd change from day to day or if his stars weren't right, or maybe that was the game that he played. If Brando plays games at least he's consistent about it. You know if you run into Brando he's gonna play mental chess with you, but if you run into Sinatra you never know what the game is.

Also in the cast was John Leyton who told me:

It wasn't a very happy movie. Sinatra arrived and left in a helicopter with all his henchmen. It was 'Frank Sinatra and Trevor Howard in ...' and there was Trevor Howard going out to the location in the car, bumping around in this old Citroën.

We've been on the set since about 8 o'clock and at about ten-thirty nobody's shot anything. And then the helicopter arrives. Out steps Frank Sinatra, everybody's ready for him in front of the cameras. Action! Camera! That's it! Cut! Print! He's back in the helicopter and back off home, and we're still standing there. I think it's understandable if Trevor was put out by this favoured treatment Sinatra got.

I've seen him get pretty bad-tempered with people. In between shots, you want to sit and relax and not get hassled, but between shots he would sit down and there would be a ring of photographers round him going click! click! click! Every now and then he would say, 'Give me ten minutes, fellas,' and they'd go away. But somebody would come back after about seven minutes and he'd be the one who gets slugged.

While Sinatra refused to associate with Peter Lawford, Sammy Davis Jnr was generous enough – and possibly courageous enough – to partner Lawford in a Swinging Sixties Buddy-Buddy caper *Salt and Pepper* (1968), directed by Richard Donner. The film was successful enough to inspire a sequel a year later, *One More Time*, directed, ironically, by Dean Martin's one-time partner Jerry Lewis.

That year, 1969, Sammy Davis Jnr married chorus girl Altovise Gore. Shortly after, he was rushed to hospital with suspected liver failure. Doctors gave him six months to live if he didn't quit drinking. With his wife's help, he did quit.

By this time Lawford had divorced Pat Kennedy and married Deborah Gould. His estrangement from Sinatra, the death of Marilyn Monroe and the assassination of John Kennedy, all in quick succession, had sent Lawford spiralling down a self-destructive path of drink and drugs. In 1974 he met the woman who was to become this third and last wife, Patricia Seaton. He was, by then, a sick man. He continued to deteriorate and underwent emergency surgery for a bleeding ulcer. In 1984 his friend of many years, Liz Taylor, tried to get him back in front of the cameras and to conquer his alcoholism. But he was too far gone and when his ulcer finally burst, he went into a coma and died on Christmas Eve 1984.

Meanwhile Davis continued to suffer with a string of health problems, including lung infections and a hip replacement. His incredible determination and immodest personality kept him at the top of his profession. But there was a secret side to Davis. When pornography star Linda Lovelace gave up her seedy career and wrote an exposé of the porn business, she related an episode in which she and another man watched a porn movie with Davis. As she gave oral sex to the other man, Davis watched fascinated, and, asking her to instruct him how to do it, took over from her.

In 1980 Davis and Dean Martin were together again in *The Cannonball Run*, a star-studded comedy headed by Burt Reynolds and directed by Hal Needham. When Reynolds and Needham embarked on the sequel, *The Cannonball Run II* in 1983, they brought Martin and Davis back to reprise their roles. Needham then figured that if he could get two Rat Packers, why couldn't he get three? So he offered Sinatra a role, he accepted and flew into Old Tucson, Arizona in his private jet and did his role in one day.

This was a vastly different Sinatra from the old days, a more mellow personality, according to Dom DeLuise, Reynold's sidekick in the picture. 'It was like the Pope came. Sinatra is the Royalty in this business. But he is very patient. He must have taken a thousand pictures with people. It's funny about a King like that. He doesn't know he's intimidating. He was sitting in a chair – we were all having our picture taken – and I mentioned that it would be good if he could stand with us, so we could all be together. But Burt turned aside and said, "Yeah, but who's going to tell him?" In the end, I told him.'

The former King Rat now spends his days raising funds for kids all over the world. In 1988 he even opened the doors of his lavish Palm Springs mansion for a Magic Carpet Weekend to raise cash for his wife Barbara's centre for sexually abused children at the nearby Eisenhower Hospital. For just £14,000 couples could count themselves among Sinatra's guests.

He and Dean Martin are the remaining members of the original Rat Pack. Sammy Davis Jnr always knew his days were numbered, but he refused to go out without a fight. Suffering from cancer of the throat, he joined Sinatra and Liza Minnelli in 1989 for a series of sellout shows. While in London he said, 'You name it and I've done it. I'd like to say I did it my way. But that line, I'm afraid, belongs to someone else.'

In May 1990 he was rushed to a Los Angeles hospital. When doctors gave up hope of any recovery, they sent him home to be with Altovise when he died. Liza Minnelli, upon hearing the news, cancelled a New York show to fly to Beverly Hills. She was one of the last people he saw before he died.

9

The Brat Pack

By the eighties the Rats had had their day. Then came the era of the Brat Pack, a bunch of young Hollywood actors who came on to the scene thinking they were God's gift to the cinema – and some of them were. As Barry Norman put it, 'There were three essential requirements to becoming a member of the Hollywood Brat Pack – you had to be successful, youthful and incredibly bratty.'

They became collectively known as the Brat Pack because, like the original Rat Pack, these young actors tended to work together as an ensemble. But, unlike the sixties originals, they tended not to play together. Which is just as well because some of them have played just a little bit too hard, landing themselves in serious trouble. The press may have labelled them all Brats, but not all of them had any great desire to raise hell and make headlines. But there were those in the pack who did.

The Brat Pack came into being sometime in the early eighties. It can possibly be traced to *Taps* in 1981. It starred Timothy Hutton (son of the late James Hutton), Sean Penn and Tom Cruise. The film itself didn't set the world alight, but critics and movie-makers were impressed with the young stars. Then in 1983 Francis Coppola, in search of a money-spinner, came up with *The Outsiders*, a story of teenage rebellion in the fifties, and cast it full of unknowns who wouldn't demand huge fees. They included Tom Cruise, Mat Dillon, Rob Lowe, Patrick Swayze, Ralph Macchio, Emilio Estevez, Diane Lane and Tom Waits. The film was a huge success, taking the familiar gang-versus-gang plot and adding some touching character studies and excellent performances all round.

Most of the young cast of both *Taps* and *The Outsiders*, with some honorary additions to the Pack, have continually worked together – though not necessarily all at the same time – in films like *Rumble Fish*, *The Breakfast Club*, *St Elmo's Fire*, and *Young Guns*.

Some of the original Brats have become a little too old to run with the Pack. Of these Tom Cruise established himself as a powerful actor and major star in *Rainman* (1989) and *Born on the Fourth of July* (1990). He became an actor to respect.

Shunning any form of respectability, however, was Sean Penn. A string of disappointing films would have finished his career but for one real talent that he displayed, and often – for making headlines. It also helped being married to bleached-blonde ball-busting pop star Madonna. He readily admitted, 'As far as audiences go, I think I'm much more famous as Madonna's husband and as somebody who hits photographers than as an actor.'

Most of his news-making troubles began in 1986 when he and Madonna embarked on a movie that never lived up to all the hype and publicity that surrounded it, *Shanghai Surprise*. The film's shooting was marked by outbursts and tantrums from Mr and Mrs Madonna (or were they Mr and Mrs Penn?), mostly involving confrontations with reporters and photographers. But it was more than just the papparazi versus the Penns. The couple went so far as to have Chris Nixon, one of the best unit publicists in the business, fired.

In an attempt to quieten things down, executive producer George Harrison arranged for a press conference in London.

He and Madonna were present. Sean Penn was conspicuous only by his absence. Madonna answered all but the unanswerable questions – 'Do you and Sean row at home? Are there any naked nuns in the film?' – with cool, defiant charm, while George Harrison, who'd been doing this sort of thing since his Beatle days, kept the whole thing on an even keel with his Liverpudlian wit and wisdom.

After all the ballyhoo, the film was a flop. Penn's next film had him in the headlines again. He was playing a cop in *Colors*. Director Dennis Hopper used real gang members and cops in minor roles, and enlisted the help of law officer Dennis Fanning, a member of CRASH – Community Resources Against Street Hoodlums. Penn was with Fanning the night they chased, and caught, the driver of a stolen car. Another night Penn was with them when they disarmed a guy who was shooting off a shotgun in the street.

Penn's role was that of a rookie cop who believes that the only way to fight violence is with violence. As an actor, Penn had a similar philosophy about the press, and when a photographer became too persistent, Penn decked him. Already under a probation order for attacking a songwriter the previous year, he found himself on another assault charge.

That wasn't the end of his troubles. He demanded a wardrobe re-fit during filming so he could wear a bullet-proof vest after receiving death threats – reportedly a dozen in one lunch break! Sean Penn was a man America was finding it hard to take to their hearts.

Some of his troubles stemmed from a devastating vodka-based cocktail called a Kamikaze. Even before he had appeared in court on a charge of assault, he was arrested on suspicion of drink-driving in his sports car. Los Angeles police handcuffed him and hauled him off to jail. For the driving offence and the assault charge Penn was thrown in the pen for two months.

Leaving the court, Penn was asked if he wished he had done things differently. 'Yes,' he replied, 'but hindsight is 20-20 vision.' Then when a photographer asked if he could take his picture, Penn said, 'Please don't, but thank you for asking.'

His only concern at that time was whether his marriage was going to be able to stand up to his time in jail. Madonna had not even appeared in court with him. Before going to prison he was allowed to go and see her, and she told him, 'I won't divorce you while you're in prison.' Famous last words.

In a past era of Hollywood, Penn would have been dumped by every studio in town. But Mike Medavoy, head of Orion Pictures and producer of *Colors* stood up for him, saying, 'Give the kid a break. Sure, he has his troubles, but he's working on them. Sean is really a very sweet guy and loaded with talent.'

When he came out of prison he set about rebuilding his life. And he had to do it without Madonna. Which was probably the best thing that happened to him. No longer 'Mr Madonna', he threw himself into filming *Judgement in Berlin* and *Casualties of War*.

Sometimes as pugnacious off-screen as he is on, Penn knows his name spells trouble in Hollywood. He said, 'I tell you, if that incident had happened to anybody but Sean Penn – *anybody* but Sean Penn – he would never have gone to jail. I mean, if somebody says, "Don't step on my blue suede shoes", and somebody comes over and steps on his blue suede shoes, what does that guy think is gonna happen to him?'

But as if one Penn wasn't enough, along came younger brother Chris who began a promising career with *Rumble Fish* and Clint Eastwood's *Pale Rider*. Then came the smash hit dance movie *Footloose*, and success and fortune went to the younger Penn's head.

'I really blew everything after *Footloose*,' he said. 'I spent a fortune on drink and drugs. I had two houses and just gambled away most of my money.'

He went on an orgy of self-destruction in 1985, after his fiancée left him when their baby daughter died just two days old. After doctors had fought to keep the baby alive throughout the troubled pregnancy, she was born prematurely with poorly developed lungs. Following her death, Chris and his girlfriend, instead of drawing closer together, fought.

When she attacked him with a 12-inch butcher's knife, he punched her, and that brought that troubled relationship to a troubled end.

Unable to get his life and work in gear, Chris Penn changed his name and for a time worked on a building site before earning good money being beaten black and blue as a prize fighter. Then he fled to Mexico to live with the family of his parents' Mexican maid. He couldn't speak Spanish and they couldn't speak English. He was on drugs and, he said, 'killing myself'.

Then he started to pull himself together, returned to Hollywood and stayed sober – except for Sundays, when he would lock himself away and drink like a fish. Other than that, he stayed teetotal for the rest of the week. Then he received an offer to appear in *Return from the River Kwai*, which took him to the steaming jungles of the Philippines. *Best of the Best* followed and he was back in business.

'Sean and I are very much alike,' he said. 'I've been through so much more trouble than Sean, but he's famous and nothing he ever does is secret. If half the things I've done became public, I might be behind bars now.

'Almost the entire world misunderstands Sean. Of course, he has his faults, but I've grown up alongside of him and, I can tell you, he's a good guy.'

Being a young star in Hollywood, especially of the Brat kind, brings pressures and suspicion from all quarters. When Matthew Broderick, from *War Games* and *Ferris Bueller's Day Off*, miraculously survived a head-on car crash in 1989 in which two women, in the other car, died, the finger of suspicion immediately fell upon him as being the cause of the fatal accident.

Broderick's girlfriend, Jennifer Grey, star of *Dirty Dancing*, escaped with minor injuries. At the moment of impact she had her head down, leaning forward to change the cassette in the car's stereo.

Broderick had to be cut from the wreckage. Unconscious

and with a fractured thigh, he was hospitalized. When he was well enough, a makeshift court was set up in the hospital for a 30-minute hearing into which Broderick hobbled on crutches. He was charged with causing death by reckless driving and faced a possible five-year sentence. He was granted bail and then discharged himself from hospital.

A team of experts was paid handsomely by Broderick to reconstruct the accident in an attempt to find out what had happened. But his innocence couldn't be proved. When the case came to court, he didn't attend, leaving his lawyers to make a dramatic plea to the jury. 'It is a tragic situation and no one will ever know exactly what happened. I am instructed to indicate that Broderick will always feel extremely upset.' Broderick had even written a letter expressing his sympathy to the victims' family.

The charge was reduced to one of careless driving and Broderick was fined £100. There was fury from John Gallagher, whose wife and mother-in-law were the fatal crash victims. 'Justice has not been done,' he complained. 'The whole thing has been a travesty. Although nothing will bring back Anna or my mother-in-law, or even ease the heartache caused by their deaths, I owe it to their memory to publicize our family's feelings at the outcome of the case. It's really incredible that in the circumstances the more serious charge was withdrawn. In my view, the facts of the accident would have justified upholding the more serious charge originally brought against Matthew Broderick.'

At the coroner's inquest, verdicts of death from multiple injuries were returned. A police officer who was at the scene of the crash said, 'Mrs Gallagher was travelling on her own side when struck by a vehicle coming from the opposite direction on her side of the road.'

Matthew Broderick did not attend the inquest. But it was, he said, 'a terrible, terrible accident. And it's something I'll remember for the rest of my life. I was badly messed up. I have no desire to be more badly hurt.'

★

It was a bit of kinky fun that had Rob Lowe making headlines. A veteran of eleven films in the space of seven years by the age of twenty-four, he found himself faced with a terrible problem. He was, he said, 'addicted to women'. This may have been no shattering revelation for any man to make if it hadn't been for the fact that in the hot steamy summer of '89 Lowe got himself laid by two girls in Atlanta, Georgia. Not particularly shocking in this day and age, perhaps, but one of the girls was only sixteen, two years below the legal age limit for having sex in Georgia – and he video-taped all the hot action, including some lesbian love-making between underage Jan Parsons and twenty-three-year-old Tara Seburt.

He'd met the girls in a nightclub in Atlanta and took them back to his hotel to make the one film he didn't expect anyone else but him to see. That video, though, was found by Jan's brother Paul, who gave the low-down on Lowe to his mother, Lena Parsons. As well as informing the police she launched a multi-million-dollar lawsuit, claiming that Lowe used his celebrity status to seduce her hairdresser daughter.

'It was just one of those quirky, naughty, wild sort of drunken things that people do from time to time,' said Lowe. 'People do it. You think people didn't Polaroid each other fifteen years ago when that was the new technology?'

Not long before all this, he had been asked how he felt about his sex-symbol image. He'd said, 'It's just a label. It doesn't make any real connection with me. It's helped my career up to a point. But it's something I'd prefer to play down now.'

He was having trouble playing it down, with a full-scale sex scandal to contend with. He had always provided the tabloids with meaty headlines because of his numerous girlfriends. From time to time he had been linked with Princess Stephanie of Monaco, Brigitte Nielson, Oliver North's former secretary Fawn Hall, model Linda Buchanan and Brooke Shields.

He was even engaged for a while to *Little House on the Prairie* star Melissa Gilbert, but she ditched him and married New York actor Bo Brinkman instead. Rob consoled himself by dating several women before embarking on a six-week fling with Princess Stephanie. 'I should have expected it to end just like it began with Stephanie – immediately,' said Rob. 'We were from two different worlds.'

When the crunch came, she left him standing on the dance floor. Other women came and went in his life after that, including Jan Parsons who would never have been heard of but for the sex-video scandal.

'In today's world you embrace every opportunity' is his philosophy, 'take every chance, shake every hand, go to every location. At some point you're gonna have something happen that you wouldn't want repeated, something that didn't work out. A scandal, if you will.'

He's convinced everyone makes sex videos. 'Show me some-one who hasn't done that and I'll show you someone who's been so sheltered they're gonna be dull.'

Lucky Rob had all criminal charges dropped, but only on the condition that he put in two years' community service, visiting schools to lecture on the dangers of drugs, talking to juvenile delinquents and visiting prisons in his home town of Drayton, Ohio. Altanta DA, Lewis Slaton, said that this was an alternat-ive to prosecution for young, non-violent first-time offenders.

But school chiefs were stunned to think that a sex offender was going to be let loose to warn children of the dangers of immoral goings-on. As one teacher put it, 'Having Rob Lowe lecturing to our children on morals is like inviting Hitler to a Jewish wedding.'

He still had that massive lawsuit to deal with. He wrote to his insurance company claiming that his personal liability policy covered him against any possible damages. They took a different view, however, and told him he wouldn't get a penny. 'We can't be responsible if he uses his celebrity status to induce females to engage in multi-party sex,' they said.

Meanwhile some enterprising video bootlegger in New York managed to acquire a copy of the tape and began selling it. 'I heard he'd made over half a million dollars,' said Lowe. 'I think that's just sick!'

By March 1990 the case took an unexpected twist when Jan Parsons, backed by her brother Paul and her divorced father, publicly opposed Jan's mum's attempts to sue Lowe. 'We want it over with,' said Paul Parsons. 'Enough harm's been done. Everybody deserves a chance.'

Although at the time of writing Lena Parsons is still intent on pursuing the lawsuit, Lowe's lawyers claim that Lena has no right to file on Jan's behalf because the divorce papers show that Jan's father has custody of her.

In May 1990 the story was circulated that Lowe's increasingly bizarre behaviour had his friends and family urging him to seek help. In an attempt to out-Flynn Errol Flynn, he was seen at a party drunkenly trying to make love to one young girl after another. Convinced he needed therapy, Lowe booked himself into the Sierra Tucson Rehabilitation Clinic in Arizona. There he was encouraged to stand up in front of other patients and describe his own particular addiction.

A good many stars have booked themselves into clinics because of drink or drug addiction. But surely there has never been a case of any Hollywood actor admitting himself for therapy because he was so badly addicted to *women*.

Whatever the truth behind that story, in July 1990 Rob Lowe showed the world that he had the same kind of concerns and cares as everyone else when he made a surprise and last-minute appearance at the Knebworth Charity Festival where Elton John and Phil Collins were among the artists performing. Offered the chance to take part, Lowe immediately took a plane from France where he was filming and flew to England. It was a last-minute dash that took him five and a half hours to reach Heathrow Airport. Then he had to wait an hour for a taxi, but made it just in time to introduce Phil Collins.

You have to hand it to Lowe. He could have stayed in France. He could have complained that they should have asked him earlier. His reason for wanting to go, he said, was because 'I had heard it was for charity and I knew Elton

John. I worked a lot with AIDS and I felt this would be good. This is the best of both worlds. You get to hear great music and help people.'

Moody Matt Dillon has managed to avoid screaming headlines. Yet he found himself treading a familiar road when he played a junkie in *Drugstore Cowboy* (1989). 'Let's just say I've done almost everything once,' he said. 'At least I never really had a drugs problem.'

Keifer Sutherland, son of Donald, managed to stear clear of drugs, 'although I have been known to let off steam occasionally,' he said. Brat Packers like Keifer Sutherland are in a sense rebels to the cause. He prefers to stay at home with his wife and two children, shunning ritzy Hollywood parties.

The Brat Pack is not exclusively male. Demi Moore, Molly Ringwald and Diane Lane head the female contingent – and they have proved a lot less excessive with their lives than some of their male colleagues. And as they each grow older and make it – or don't – through the nineties, the Pack is already well on its way to becoming just another part of Hollywood folklore. It was a term that never pleased its membership anyway.

'I used to bridle a bit when all it did was add to the confusion over who we all were as individuals,' said Rob Lowe. 'It was easier for the press to write "Brat Pack" than to write Tom, or Matthew, or Rob or whoever. But at least it did get us written about. And now we've all managed to carve out or own identities, and to be recognized for our own distinctive bodies of work.'

10

Hollywood Hoods

Gangsters were there at the beginning when Hollywood began under the gun. Hoodlums and gunmen were put on the payroll of the Motion Picture Patents Company to enforce the self-imposed law of an illegal and feared trust. Wall Street banker and Biograph representative Jeremiah J Kennedy, the spokesman for the MPPC, decided that any independent film makers who refused to pay the necessary fees for patents as well as purchase a licence would be dealt with severely, and not altogether legally.

The MPPC was quite clearly a 'trust'. It was set up in 1908 after a court decision upheld Thomas Edison's claims to ownership of certain motion picture patents. Jeremiah Kennedy suggested to Edison that he join with Biograph, which owned the patent on the movie camera, to form the Trust. Vitagraph and Armat contributed their patents, thus earning them a cut, and licences were issued to Essanay, Kalem, Selig, Kleine, Lubin, Pathé and Melies.

Carl Laemmle of the IMP Company, received 289 lawsuits from the Trust in the space of three years, and in a move to counteract their control, Laemmle joined with other independent film makers to form the Motion Picture

Distributing and Sales Company. Injunctions were brought against the independents, and when that had no impact, the gangsters were sent in. To combat them, the independents hired their own gangsters. Some companies moved to the West Coast to escape the Trust so gunmen were sent to California, where they found themselves shooting it out with the cowboys hired to protect the besieged studios.

All over America battles raged in the various factions' efforts to take control of the film industry. In Chicago opposing unions claiming to represent the motion picture operators brought in gangsters to shoot it out and cause riots in the streets.

It was all further complicated when the Motion Picture Distributing and Sales Company had internal conflicts and producer Pat Powers formed the Universal Film Manufacturing Company – Universal Pictures had been born. However, Carl Laemmle soon took control of Universal and when the New York Motion Picture Company withdrew from the parent company, Laemmle sent gunmen to take over the dissident film company's laboratory. The men at the lab had been forewarned and armed guards were set up. Laemmle's gunmen were driven off in a hail of bullets.

By 1913 things had really hotted up. Cecil B De Mille was filming *The Squaw Man* in Hollywood, and, with the Trust trying to drive him out of business, he took precautions, as Jesse Lasky Jnr recounted.

My father told me that De Mille had a revolver on him when he arrived in Hollywood because after stopping off at Flagstaff he and my father had found themselves in the middle of a war between the cattlemen and the sheepmen, and De Mille wasn't taking any chances. As well as the revolver, he also kept a wolf which he had acquired for the film, and it made for an excellent guard dog.

One day De Mille arrived at his studio and found that gangsters from the Trust had already got there and had destroyed the negative. Fortunately, De Mille had another copy or he would have had to start filming *The Squaw Man* all over again.

Next they started sending him letters saying, 'Get out of town' or words to that effect, threatening him with death if he continued making films. What he did was to buy himself a bigger and more powerful revolver. Then while he was coming home one evening through a place called Cahuenga Pass, he was shot at by someone, hired obviously by the Trust, and he felt the bullet whizz just past by his head. He was lucky not to have been killed.

There were some in the Trust who believed that film making would prove to be merely a passing fad and they were intent on milking it for all it was worth before the well ran dry. But the well positively overflowed and the independents went from strength to strength, eventually breaking the Trust.

The movie business no longer needed the services of the gangsters, especially as a group of prominent men in Hollywood set themselves up as the 'Combination', paying off the police and federal agents to the tune of $50,000,000 a year for turning a blind eye to various illegal activities, including gambling and prostitution.

The Combination held its breath when, in 1927, Chicago mob boss Al Capone rode into town. They feared that he was planning to move in with a protection racket. Detectives paid Capone a visit and he told them that he'd just heard so much about California that he wanted to see it for himself. It appears to have been a remarkably amiable meeting, during which Capone offered the 'tecs a drink, assuring them that he would be returning home the following day. The next day he was on the train heading back to Chicago, but within the next seven years, Capone would be sending back some of his 'boys'.

The year before Al Capone's first visit to Tinsel Town, a new face had arrived on the scene. He wasn't a member of the Mafia. But he was one of the country's most prominent, and respected, bootleggers, Joseph P Kennedy. A Harvard graduate, Kennedy had decided at college that he would be a millionaire by the age of thirty-five. At twenty-five he was Boston's youngest bank president. Prohibition provided him with another way of achieving his goal. But he wasn't one for providing poisonous wood alcohol. He imported the finest Scotch and Irish whiskies and French champagne, which he stored in and distributed from secret warehouses on the East and West Coasts.

He had little interest in the film industry, save to provide Hollywood with the best that bootleg could offer. But when a small-town banker friend of his told how he had invested $120,000 in the Lon Chaney film *The Miracle Man* and earned back $3,000,000, Kennedy realized that the movie business was a pie he should put one or two fingers into. From his new headquarters in New York, he bought a chain of movie theatres. Then he decided to move into the picture-making business and bought a British studio, before purchasing, in 1926, sight unseen, the Hollywood-based Film Booking Offices of America Inc. Studio.

When he took his first look around his new enterprise, he realized that the studio lacked the prestige of the majors. It turned out a feature a week, mainly westerns which the big city picture palaces wouldn't play – until Kennedy used his charming and winning manner to persuade a major theatre to show a Fred Thomson cowboy picture, which proved an enormous success.

Kennedy then moved in on the Keith-Albee-Orpheum theatre empire, buying the circuit and then selling it for a huge profit with which he acquired Pathé Exchange, later merging the company into RKO. He also embarked on a love affair with Gloria Swanson and produced many of her pictures. But one theatre circuit he had his eyes on evaded him. Greek-born Alexander Pantages ran one of the two biggest chains on the West Coast. In 1920 the great Art Deco designer B Marcus Priteca had created the beautiful Los Angeles Pantages Theatre. Then, one day in August 1929, something happened at the theatre that, initially, seemed to have no connection whatsoever with Joe Kennedy.

Teenager Eunice Pringle had bought a ticket and then found her way up to the office of Pantages on the mezzanine level. A little later the audience heard screams and a young man working at the theatre went to investigate. He found Eunice on the mezzanine screaming hysterically. She collapsed in his arms and, pointing at Alexander Pantages in his office, accused Pantages of raping her in the cleaner's closet which was just opposite his office.

A traffic policeman was soon on the scene and the small middle-aged Greek entrepreneur said to him, 'Can't you see, she's trying to frame me.'

Eunice told the police that she was a dancer and had come to the theatre to see if Pantages was interested in her act. The Greek tycoon had then thrown her into the cleaner's closet, torn her panties and raped her.

At the preliminary hearing, the demurely dressed Eunice told the DA, 'He said he wanted me for his sweetheart. I told him I was not interested in sweethearts, I was interested in work, but he continued his advances. He seemed to go crazy. He clapped his hand over my mouth. He bit me on the breast.' She explained that she had fainted and when she came to she was in the closet with her dress up and Pantages raping her.

Pantages insisted that Eunice had visited him on several occasions but he had refused to book her because her act was 'too suggestive'. He was booked and sent for trial before the Los Angeles Superior Court. Eunice again appeared demurely dressed. Her hair was tied in a bow. She looked no older than thirteen. The jury was immediately impressed with her.

They were not impressed, however, by Pantages's broken English and what they considered to be European arrogance. He told them that the girl had 'raped herself', tearing her own clothing. He told them bluntly that there was no need for him to molest a girl in a cleaner's cupboard with sex so readily available throughout Hollywood.

His lawyer was one Jerry Geisler, then relatively unknown. (In years to come his clients would include Errol Flynn,

Charlie Chaplin, Lana Turner's daughter Cheryl, and Robert Mitchum.) Before the court recessed, Geisler requested that Eunice return the following day wearing the same clothing she'd worn on the day of the attack. She returned the following day in a red, low-cut dress, looking like a seductive woman. Geisler wanted the court to examine Eunice's moral background, but such testimony was barred on the grounds that the morals of a minor were not an issue since a minor was legally incapable of giving assent in a sex case.

Pantages was found guilty and sentenced to 50 years in prison. Geisler filed an appeal, arguing that to exclude testimony about the morals of Eunice Pringle was prejudicial to his client. He took the case to the California Supreme Court and succeeded in opening a new trial in 1931 in which the court allowed that any relevant evidence was admissible, creating a precedent for the adjudication of California rape cases (very handy for Geisler when he came to defend Errol Flynn on similar charges).

When Geisler got Eunice to admit that her dancing skills included doing a full split, he and his associate Jake Ehrlich asked the jury to consider that an athletic youngster with Eunice's strength and abilities could easily fight off a small middle-aged man such as Pantages. Then Geisler and Ehrlich re-enacted the rape in court, with Geisler portraying Pantages and Ehrlich as Eunice. They hoped to convince the jury that it was impossible for the rape to have taken place in the closet as described by Eunice.

Then Geisler played his trump card, using the court's permission to introduce evidence regarding the morals of this minor. He contended that Eunice had not only conspired with her agent, Nick Dunaev, to compromise Pantages, but that the two of them had cohabited in Bungalow 45 at Moonbeam Glen Bungalow Court. To verify this, Geisler introduced the testimony of an elderly lady who managed the Bungalows. The old lady identified Eunice and her agent as the former occupants of Bungalow 45.

Pantages was found not guilty and released.

Years later, on her deathbed, Eunice Pringle made a startling confession. She said that it had been Joseph Kennedy who had masterminded the frame-up in the hope of destroying Pantages and acquiring his empire.

In 1934 there was a threat to another theatre chain, this one belonging to Barney Balaban and his partner Sam Katz, who had opened their first theatre in Chicago in 1908. In 1917 they introduced ice-cooled refrigeration as a primitive form of air-conditioning into their theatres. They found themselves victims of a shake-down by George Browne and Willie Bioff, two racketeers who had taken over the local Chicago branch of the International Alliance of Theatrical State Employees, an organization encompassing some thousand unions in North America representing members in every branch of film production, distribution and exhibition.

Balaban tried to bribe Browne with a $150 a week payoff not to raise the salaries of his theatre employees. Browne accepted but when Bioff heard he went straight to Balaban, rejected the bribe and demanded a $50,000 payment. Balaban refused to pay. Consequently, films being shown at their theatres were blacked out, or run backwards, and furious patrons were demanding their money back. Balaban and Katz had no choice but to avoid eventual ruin by handing over $50,000 to Browne and Bioff.

The two racketeers couldn't help boasting how easy it was to shake down these entrepreneurs, and word that they were going to make a fortune by threatening a projectionists' strike throughout Chicago reached the ears of Frank 'The Enforcer' Nitti, Al Capone's lieutenant. He sent 'Cherry Nose' Gioe to tell Browne and Bioff that the syndicate was cutting in with them. As proof of how serious they were, the leader of the Projectionists' Union and the President of the Janitors' Union were both blasted away. Browne and Bioff didn't argue.

Frank Nitti wanted George Browne elected as the national puppet President of the IATSE and conferred with Paul 'The Waiter' Lucca, Lepke Buchalter and Lucky Luciano (possibly the biggest of all the mafiosi) on how best to 'convince' the unions' members to vote for the right man.

When Browne won hands down, he appointed Bioff as international representative and sent him to Hollywood. About that time Lucky Luciano decided to move his illegal gambling enterprise into California. He owned casinos all over America and, as Hollywood became a land flowing with milk and money during the twenties and early thirties, he decided in 1935 to move in. Looking for a suitable establishment from which to run his prospective casino, he approached Thelma Todd, the 'Ice-cream Blonde', who ran her own roadside café.

The mobster gave Thelma an offer she shouldn't refuse – she would bring her famous friends to spend their considerable wealth in the secret casino which would be installed upstairs. Todd was a gutsy girl, not unlike the characters she played in comedies, often with Laurel and Hardy. She led a fast, fun-filled life, fed on a staple diet of parties, pills, sex and spirits. She was plucky enough to stand up to the Mafia and turned Lucky Luciano down.

Not long after, she was found dead from carbon monoxide poisoning, slumped in her car parked in its garage. A struggle had taken place; there was blood on her face, dress and mink coat. An inquest was unable to determine her manner of death and delivered an open verdict. Thelma's lawyer, however, pressed for a second inquest at which he would prove his theory; in turning down Lucky Luciano, she had sealed her fate. Hal Roach, to whom Thelma had been under contract, broke into a cold sweat and persuaded the attorney they might all live a little longer if he dropped his accusation.

Thelma Todd's death remained an open verdict. But the whole of Hollywood knew that she had been 'knocked off by gangsters', as Clark Gable put it.

Meanwhile Bioff was making inroads, bringing an end to the 'Combination' and threatening to bring the whole movie business to a halt simply by bringing the projectionists out on strike. In New York, Bioff demanded $2,000,000 from Nicholas Schenck, president of Loew's Inc., which was MGM's parent company. Refusing to pay, Schenck met with

Sidney Kent, president of Twentieth Century-Fox, and they decided to stand against the racketeers. But when Bioff made it clear that he would shut every studio in Hollywood with strikes, they came to a compromise and $75,000 was handed over.

Bioff installed himself as the one and only agent through which MGM, Fox and Warner Bros must purchase their raw film stock, earning 7 per cent commission for the syndicate. By now Bioff was up against competition from other racketeers. Word had reached the New York mob that Chicago had sent in someone to shake down Hollywood, so Bugsy Siegel and half a dozen other New York gangsters were despatched West. Siegel arrived to find his good friend, George Raft, waiting for him.

Of all the screen gangsters, George Raft came the closest to his screen image. During his teens he and Siegel had found numerous ways of making money within the confines of their Hell's Kitchen ghetto. Raft boxed in the prize-ring, winning fifteen of his twenty-two bouts and 'retiring' with his Valentino looks intact. He took to the dance halls as a gigolo, raking in the money from lonely, older and wealthy women. He danced his way to London and back to New York and began earning legitimate money from dancing on the Broadway stage with partner Elsie Pilcer.

Siegel had been a lot less elegant than Raft in making a name for himself. A rapist, burglar and all-round punk, he began pushing heroin for Lucky Luciano. During Prohibition he ran bootleg liquor, a sideline Raft delved in away from his stage work.

Raft once said, 'If I had any ambition, it was to be a big shot in my pal Owney Maddon's liquor mob. I had a gun in my pocket, and I was cocky because I was working for the gang boss of New York.'

When Maddon supplied a 'protection' crew for cowgirl movie star Texas Guinan's nightclub, Raft was included. Texas was impressed with Raft's good looks and took him to Hollywood to play a small part in her film *Queen of the Night*

Clubs (1929). Further roles followed, usually as a gangster. In 1932 he appeared with Paul Muni in Howard Hawks's classic *Scarface*, which was based on the nefarious activities of Al Capone. During the making of the film Capone himself visited the set. Hawks invited him to see the rushes, which delighted the real Scarface, and when Hawks visited Chicago some time after, Capone gave a party in his honour and presented him with a miniature machine-gun.

Raft had become a major star at Warner Bros by 1936 when Siegel turned up representing the New York Mob. Raft arranged for Siegel to rent opera singer and movie star Lawrence Tibbett's mansion.

While Bioff was threatening to pull the plug on the studios by bringing technicians of every type out on strike, Siegel specialized in 'representing' the thousands of extras that Hollywood could then afford for crowd scenes. To ensure that the extras would turn up for work, the studios made payoffs to Siegel who earned half a million dollars in one year from this alone. Bugsy also had a nice line in drugs, gambling and prostitution.

Through Raft, Siegel met and tried to befriend numerous stars including Clark Gable, Jean Harlow and Cary Grant. They were all careful not to offend Siegel, and some were even enchanted by his immense charm and filmstar looks. He paid special attention to Jean Harlow who was no stranger to the underworld. A few years earlier she had spent a good deal of time with Longie Zwillman, one of America's top bootleggers. He was obsessed with Harlow and gave her a platinum charm bracelet on which hung tiny objects including a pig (symbolic of her eating habits) and a man of the world (representing him).

Now she became the object of Siegel's desire, although she rejected his constant advances. Her stepfather, Marino Bello, began getting involved in Siegel's activities. Bello had swindled his stepdaughter out of a vast amount of money, claiming he had invested it in various enterprises, including a Mexican gold mine. All these enterprises, like the gold mine, were fictitious. Bello also claimed to have been associated with the likes of Capone and Johnny Torrio. Siegel gave Bello a job or two to the dismay of Harlow with whom Siegel remained infatuated until her death in 1937.

In 1939 word reached Siegel's ears that a stool-pigeon, Harry Greenberg, was about to start singing like a bird to federal officers. Hitman Allie Tannenbaum silenced Greenberg permanently and Siegel was arrested, suspected of masterminding the hit. He called in Jerry Geisler to defend him in court. It no doubt went in Siegel's favour that he had generously donated $50,000 to District Attorney Dockweiler's re-election campaign. He was subsequently set free.

For a while Siegel dallied with the Countess Di Frasso, an East Coast heiress who had previously married into the Italian aristocracy before making a splash in Hollywood society. Siegel caught her on the rebound from Gary Cooper. He even found himself a wife somewhere but came to lavish all his loving attention on small-time actress and big-time gangster's moll, Virginia Hill. Before coming to Hollywood Virginia had graduated from the vice dens of New York to lavish parties of Lucky Luciano and Frank Costello where she played the part of 'hostess'.

In 1941 she arrived in Hollywood to see if she could make it as an actress, and promptly took up with Bugsy. He pulled a few of Sam Goldwyn's strings and landed her a small role in *Ball of Fire* opposite Gary Cooper and Barbara Stanwyck. Siegel and his moll were among the stars at the glittering première.

As for Bioff, he found he didn't scare everyone in Hollywood. In what may have been a futile effort to win over George Raft, he suggested shaking down Warners to give Raft a better deal. Bioff could arrange for a light to fall on to James Gagney's head on the set of *Each Dawn I Die* (1938) if Warners failed to comply. The plan was abandoned. Cagney was Raft's friend. It was an unforgivable gaff and may well have set in motion the wheels that led to Bioff's downfall, possibly with Siegel's aid.

There was opposition to Bioff from Arthur Ungar, editor of the *Daily Variety*, Robert Montgomery, president of the Screen Actors Guild, and columnist Westbrook Pegler. They instigated an investigation into Bioff's dubious past and private detectives discovered that Bioff had served time for running a brothel. Pegler courageously published the findings.

Perhaps sensing the end was near for this particular mafioso agent, Cecil B De Mille stood up to him (metaphorically speaking, since De Mille was flat on his back at the time) during the filming of *Union Pacific* (1939). This was the first De Mille film that Jesse Lasky Jnr worked on as screen playwright.

De Mille was working frantically and collapsed from overwork and a troubled prostate gland [he told me]. He underwent an emergency operation and was ordered to bed for two weeks. But being Cecil B De Mille, he continued to direct the film flat on his back from his stretcher.

A gangster running the technicians' union came to him and said that unless he paid however much money, De Mille might find himself the victim of an accident. I wasn't there to see this, but I understand that De Mille rose up like the Pillar of Fire from *The Ten Commandments* from his bed and said, 'I've been shot at more than I'd care to remember, and threatened with death. When I first came out to Hollywood the Trust sent small-time gangsters like you to kill me, but as you see, I'm still alive. Do you know why I'm still alive?' 'No,' said the gangster. 'Because,' said De Mille, 'I've got God on my side.' Now, De Mille was a greater actor than many of the actors he hired, and he must have been in great pain but he remained standing and he said, 'I was told I would never stand again. But as you can see, God has made me stand. Do you honestly think you can succeed where all others have failed? I defy you to cause an "accident". God defies you. Now get out of here.'

And he got out of there and nothing happened to De Mille.

The FBI were now on to Bioff, investigating a $100,000 cheque made payable to him and signed by Joseph Schenck who felt compelled to claim that it had merely been a loan. Others, however, were prepared to testify that Bioff was extorting huge sums from the major studios, and Bioff and Browne were charged before a federal grand jury in 1941. Browne was sentenced to eight years, Bioff to ten.

Doing his time in Alcatraz, Bioff named several Chicago gangsters who led the syndicate, including Frank Nitti. Nitti shot himself before he could be arrested. When Bioff was released, he changed his name to Willie Nelson and settled in Arizona. In 1955 he was killed when his car mysteriously exploded.

Once Bioff was taken out of circulation in Hollywood, Siegel became the authorities' next target. With studio heads still unwilling to testify against him, the law only managed to indict him on a bookmaking charge late in 1941. The authorities failed to make the charges stick and Siegel was released.

George Raft had stepped forward as a character witness. 'I've known Mr Siegel for twenty years,' he'd told the court. 'We have been friends for a long, long time.' Siegel had few remaining friends, even among the Mafia. He'd trodden on too many gangster toes on his way up.

He still had an ally in Lucky Luciano who, from exile in Italy, sent tons of Carrara marble to the sleepy town of Las Vegas in the Nevada desert, where Siegel was building a huge hotel which would house the biggest casino in the country. The Flamingo opened for Christmas 1946. Siegel had convinced investors to pour $6,000,000 into the project and they expected a quick return. But business was slow to start with and Siegel was intent on keeping all initial profits for himself.

Virginia grew bored. Her film career was going nowhere

and Siegel was obsessed with developing Las Vegas, where they were now living. They had been secretly married in 1946, but in the spring of 1947 she walked out on him and headed back to Hollywood where she rented a huge Moorish mansion. She was about to leave for France with a young French lover when Siegel turned up and begged her to change her mind. She told him she would consider it – while she was in Europe. Siegel stayed alone in her house where, on 20 June, he was shot to death by hitmen hired by the 'investors' who were tired of waiting for their returns.

There was only a small gathering who came to see him buried at Beth Olsam Cemetery. Not a single movie star turned up for the funeral. Not even George Raft who was no longer the big noise in Hollywood.

The year Siegel died, Lucky Luciano was in Havana, running the Mafia's activities in Cuba, where, according to Kitty Kelley's controversial biography *His Way*, he was visited by Frank Sinatra. It was meetings like this one that sparked off years of speculation as to Sinatra's actual involvement with the Mafia. Despite futile attempts by some to prove that he has been actively involved with organized crime, Sinatra has associated not only with mobsters, but also with presidents and kings without ever being a politician or a member of a royal family.

Throughout his career Sinatra made many friends who were members of the mob, including Salvatore (Sam) Giancana, Al Capone's successor in Chicago, where he controlled the protection rackets, prostitution, narcotics, loan sharks, extortioners, counterfeiters and gambling. Sinatra never referred to Giancana or any other mobsters as 'Mafia'. They were always 'the Boys' or 'the Outfit'. When Sinatra finished his nightclub act with *My Kind of Town Chicago Is*, it was, according to Peter Lawford, a tribute to Giancana. Lawford described Giancana as 'an awful guy with a gargoyle face and weasel nose. I couldn't stand him, but Frank idolized him.'

Because Sinatra was a friend of Giancana, nobody dared to mess with Sinatra. Giancana respected him and when the Mafia boss wanted to arrange a meeting with Attorney-General, Bobby Kennedy, to discuss cutting down on the FBI surveillance, he sent an emissary to tell a Justice Department Official, 'If Bobby agrees, tell him to get in touch with Sinatra to set it up.'

Sinatra also set Giancana up with numerous women – as he did for John Kennedy, son of Joseph P Kennedy and President of the United States of America, one of them being, as mentioned earlier, Marilyn Monroe, of whom Sinatra was exceptionally fond.

Kennedy's friendship with Sinatra worried some of the Democratic Party leaders and lawyers in brother Bobby's Justice Department. They felt that Sinatra could be a political liability and so the President agreed to Bobby assigning agents to check out Sinatra's connections. 'Just find out whether Frank could be embarrassing to us,' said JFK. He enjoyed his friendship with Sinatra and didn't want to jeopardize it. Sinatra had supported him in his campaign and the President was always grateful for that.

Henry Peterson, deputy chief of the Organized Crime section, began checking through the FBI files, collating the information J Edgar Hoover had amassed on Sinatra and almost everyone else who was famous. A few agents were ordered to dig up some current information on Sinatra's activities in Las Vegas and Chicago. Three reports were drawn up throughout 1962. The final report, completed on 3 August, concluded:

> Sinatra has had a long and wide association with hoodlums and racketeers which seems to be continuing. The nature of Sinatra's work may, on occasion, bring him into contact with underworld figures but this cannot account for his friendship and/or financial involvement with people such as Joe and Rocco Fischetti, cousins of Al Capone, Paul Emilio D'Amanto, John Formosa and Sam Giancana, all of whom are on our list of racketeers. No other entertainer appears to be mentioned nearly so often with racketeers.

Available information indicates not only that Sinatra is associated with each of the above-named racketeers but that they apparently maintain contact with one another. This indicates a possible community of interest involving Sinatra and racketeers in Illinois, Indiana, New Jersey, Florida and Nevada.

Bobby Kennedy felt this sufficient to prove Sinatra a political liability to his brother and persuaded him to dissociate himself from the singer. The President was obliged to cancel plans to be a guest at Sinatra's house (which action led to the bust-up between Sinatra and Peter Lawford). However, the President privately pursued his friendship with Sinatra who was thus able to maintain his affiliations with both the President of America and the Godfather of Chicago. He even furnished them both with the same woman, Judith Campbell, who found herself in the remarkable situation of having simultaneous affairs with leaders of the White House and the Underworld.

Around this time Sinatra came to the aid of George Raft who had been having a rough time, and gave him a role in his Rat Pack picture *Ocean's Eleven*. Raft had become a has-been, relegated to B-movies. He'd tried his luck in Europe where he made a number of films during the fifties. He was also seen on numerous occasions in Cuba, where he owned a casino in Havana, which no doubt had the support of the Mafia, which controlled the island's prosperous gambling business.

It was his link with the Mafia that caused him trouble in 1957 when he went to Britain to make *Morning Call*, which he walked out of because he didn't like the script. He chose instead to stay on and make *Women of the Night*, but found his work permit revoked by the British Government who were suspicious of his underworld connections. He denied any such association.

Out of work on both sides of the Atlantic, he complained to the *Sunday Express*, 'This is a cruel business if you're sensitive. And Hollywood's a cruel place. The moment you start slipping nobody wants to know you.'

His gambling casino helped to keep him in pocket, but disaster struck when in 1959 Castro successfully launched his revolution in Cuba, kicking out the Mafia and closing all the casinos, including Raft's, without any compensation.

Raft made a few cameo appearances back in Hollywood, including *Some Like it Hot* (1959) and Sinatra's *Ocean's Eleven* (1960). In 1965 he faced a further blow when the American Government slammed him with a demand for back tax. He fled to France to make a couple of awful movies and then decided to settle in Britain to run the casino he had opened in London.

He did go back to the US, but when he wanted to return to Britain he was refused entry by the British Government because of his alleged underworld associations. Again he vehemently denied the allegations and tried for many years to gain permission to enter the UK. But his dubious past had caught up with him and he was forced to remain in America until he died in 1980 at the remarkable age of eighty-five.

Frank Sinatra now devotes a great deal of his time to raising money for needy children and supporting his lovely wife Barbara's centre for sexually abused children. Journalists Sandra White and Ian Black, who attended a Magic Carpet Weekend With The Sinatras (when the Sinatra Palm Springs mansions was opened to those willing to part with huge sums of money for Barbara Sinatra's charity) reported that 'Sinatra today is gentle, caring, good fun and tolerant'. Hardly the image of one mixing with racketeers. It would seem, then, that with Raft's death died the last remnant of any close links the Mafia had with Hollywood. And if there are any Mafia activities going on in Tinsel Town, *I'm* certainly not going to be the one to try and find out about them.

Index